# GREAT GOALIES OF PRO HOCKEY

For the men who stand in front of the net, pro hockey is a grueling game. As their teams' last line of defense, goalies must brave speeding pucks, flashing skate-blades and deadly sticks. Exciting profiles of ten great goaltenders tell how—and why—they do it. Included are Tony Esposito, Jacques Plante, Johnny Bower, Glenn Hall, Ken Dryden, Bill Durnan, Terry Sawchuk, Gerry Cheevers, Gump Worsley and Vladislav Tretiak.

# GREAT GOALIES OF PRO HOCKEY

## BY FRANK ORR

illustrated with photographs

RANDOM HOUSE    PRO HOCKEY LIBRARY    NEW YORK

Copyright © 1973 by Random House, Inc.

All rights reserved under International and Pan-American Copyright Conventions. Published in the United States by Random House, Inc., New York, and simultaneously in Canada by Random House of Canada Limited, Toronto.

Manufactured in the United States of America

Library of Congress Cataloging in Publication Data

Orr, Frank. Great goalies of pro hockey. (Pro hockey library)
CONTENTS: Tony Esposito, time-bomb.—Jacques Plante, the innovater.—Johnny Bower, the reluctant goalie. [etc.] 1. Hockey—Biography—Juvenile literature. [1. Hockey—Biography] I. Title.
GV848.5.A1067 1973      796.9′62′0922 [B] [920]      73–5896
ISBN 0-394-82539-X                   ISBN 0-394-92539-4 (lib. bdg.)

# Contents

# Introduction

The big league hockey goaltender has one of the most difficult and demanding jobs in sport. Standing on a sheet of ice, he must keep a rubber puck from entering a net six feet wide and four feet high. He wears mattress-like pads on his legs, a cushion on his chest and if he wishes, a protective mask on his face. In his outsized gloves he holds a heavy stick.

But even with all that equipment, the goalie's task is pure punishment. He must put his body between the goal and the puck, which may be traveling 115 miles per hour. He must dive into player pile-ups, among skates that slash and sticks that cut and bruise.

But physical hazards are only part of the story. The goalie also faces great mental stress.

As one NHL coach explained, "The pressure of the job gets to every goalie in some way. Sure, that strain reaches the players in other positions, too. But they aren't out there on their own, standing alone the way a goalie is."

Or as veteran goalie Jacques Plante put it, "How would you like it in your job if you made a little goof, a red light came on behind you and 17,000 people yelled, 'Get that stupid bum out of there'?"

Yet with all the difficulties, countless young boys dream of becoming professional goalies. What makes them choose this grueling job?

Often in boys' pick-up games, a youngster who isn't a strong skater may be assigned to play goal. Plante became a goalie because a childhood asthma condition prevented him from skating strenuously in the icy cold.

As a youngster, Johnny Bower couldn't afford a pair of skates so he became a netminder, the only position he could play without them. After years in the National Hockey League, Bower still wasn't quite sure why he did it. "Sometimes after facing Bobby Hull's shot," he admitted, "I wonder if I have all my brains."

Goalies fall into two main categories—those who rely on technique and those who rely on reflexes. The technicians "play the angles," positioning themselves between the attackmen and the goal to reduce the net openings to a minimum. Thus, if a shooter tries to avoid the goalie, he is likely to miss the net, too. Most technicians are stand-up netminders like Montreal's Bill Durnan, who dropped to the ice only as a last resort.

Reflex goalies, on the other hand, count on

their quick reactions. They often force the shooter to make the first move, then get a glove, pad, stick or part of their body in front of the shot. Glenn Hall was one of hockey's great reflex goalies.

Whatever style they use, however, all great goalies have several qualities in common: lightning speed, nerves of steel, poise and experience. The men who guard the nets are unique individuals, and the stories of the best of them are told here.

They range from Bill Durnan, the exceptional Montreal goalie of the 1940s to Tony Esposito, the unorthodox Chicago netminder of the '70s. Also included is Vladislav Tretiak, the remarkable young backstop of the Soviet National Team.

Tretiak is technically an amateur, yet his exceptional work in the 1972 series against the professionals of Team Canada was a highlight of the historic series. With further competition between North American and Soviet teams, he seems sure to become an important international sports star.

# TONY ESPOSITO
## Time-Bomb

Tony Esposito looked like a bomb that was about to explode. While the national anthem played he fidgeted in front of the Chicago Black Hawks' net. An awkward figure in his bulky goaltender's equipment, Esposito jiggled from one foot to the other, shook his shoulders and, holding his gloves, stick and mask in one hand, repeatedly ran the other hand through his dark, curly hair. His face was drawn in tight lines, which clearly revealed the strain and pressure of his profession.

The anthem ended and Esposito retreated to the goal crease where he slid from side to side, pushing down heavily on his skate blades to

9

smooth out the bumps on the ice. Even when his teammates crowded around him to slap his pads in the traditional pregame "good-luck" gesture, Tony Esposito never relaxed.

As soon as the game started, though, all of Esposito's nervousness seemed to disappear. Suddenly he became a padded acrobat—diving, scrambling and kicking to stop shots. He glided away from his protective crease to challenge the opposing shooters. He crouched low to halt the shots which were screened from view by the players in front of him. Sometimes he misplayed a shot, then saved a goal at the last second by knocking the puck away with a glove or a pad.

It wasn't very often that his remarkable reflexes failed him. But when a shot did get by him and the red light flashed, Esposito became the picture of total dejection. His entire body seemed to slump. If he was down on the ice when the goal was scored, he remained frozen in that position for several agonizing seconds, shaking his head in disgust or disappointment. Often he kicked his goal stick or banged it against the post, angry with himself for making a mistake even when it seemed clear that no one could have stopped the shot.

Tony Esposito was one of the most intense competitors in the National Hockey League and one of its very best goalies. Still, he worried and brooded, and was often sullen and uncommunicative. He was not a classic stylist like Jacques

**Chicago's Tony Esposito dives for the puck in a game against St. Louis.**

Plante, the dean of NHL netminders. He was not a stand-up goalie who smoothly played the angles. He was a scrambler—a goalie who relied on his extraordinary reflexes to make up for his lack of polished technique.

But Esposito stopped the puck effectively, and for a goaltender that was all that really mattered. How he did it was of little consequence. Tony entered the NHL as a first-string goalie in the 1969–70 season and recorded 15 shutouts as a rookie. In two of his first three seasons he won the Vezina Trophy as the top NHL goalie.

One explanation for Tony's intense drive may have had something to do with his brother Phil. Although Tony had moved to the front ranks of NHL goalies, Phil got most of the attention, scoring 76 goals in 1970–71 and 66 more in 1971–72. With competition like that, Tony had to be good just to keep up in his own family.

The Esposito brothers began their hockey competition by the time they learned to read. Using cut-down hockey sticks and a rolled-up wool sock for a puck, they played "hockey" games in the basement of their home. Even then, Tony was the goalie, and Phil was the shooter.

"Every Canadian kid wants to shoot the puck, and he needs someone to shoot it at," said Phil Esposito. "I was a year older than Tony, so I did the shooting. Tony probably didn't like it, but he didn't have much choice."

"Phil and I always were sort of rivals in a friendly way," Tony recalled. "No matter what game we played, he was trying to score and I was trying to stop him. We had some very competitive table hockey games when we were kids, too."

Both brothers progressed through minor age-group hockey in Sault Ste. Marie, Ontario, just across the Mackinac Strait from northern Michigan. But in their late teens, they took separate paths which eventually led to the same place—the NHL. Phil traveled the traditional route through the fast Junior A leagues, while Tony accepted a hockey scholarship at the Michigan Institute of Technology.

"I lost a little interest in playing hockey in my teens," Tony explained. "I wasn't too keen on Junior A hockey. But when the scholarship offer came, I took it because I wanted to get an education. I had no idea of a professional hockey career at that time."

Tony successfully combined education and hockey at Michigan Tech. He earned second-team All-America honors in 1964–65 and was named to the first team the following season. Although Michigan was playing in the tough Western College Hockey Association conference, Esposito surrendered only 130 goals in 51 games during three seasons of varsity competition.

In his sophomore year, the Montreal Canadiens had secured Esposito's professional rights by placing his name on their negotiation list. In 1967, Tony graduated from Michigan Tech with a degree in business administration. By this time, he had reconsidered hockey as a career and signed a professional contract with the Montreal organization. The young goalie was assigned to the Vancouver Canucks of the Western Hockey League for the 1967–68 season.

Tony's rookie year in pro hockey was a difficult one. The Canucks had a weak team, which was stuck in the Western League basement for the entire season. But even though Esposito was bombarded with shots in most games, he managed to maintain a respectable 3.20 goals-against average in 61 games.

"That season, I found out that I didn't enjoy losing very much," Esposito said. "The season was very long because we had such a bad team, but I learned a great deal, especially from Jim Gregory [the Vancouver coach who later became general manager of the Toronto Maple Leafs]."

The next season the Canadiens sent Esposito to the Houston Apollos, their farm team in the Central Hockey League. But when Montreal's regular goalies Gump Worsley and Rogatien Vachon were injured in midseason, Esposito was brought up to Montreal to replace them. Tony made the most of that opportunity, proving he was ready for big league duty. In 13 NHL games, he had a 2.73 average and two shutouts.

By the 1969–70 season Worsley and Vachon

were back in action, and Tony returned to Houston. The Canadiens protected Worsley and Vachon in the 1969 draft, but they didn't protect Tony. Luckily, Tony had made a good impression on the Canadiens' NHL rivals, and the Chicago Black Hawks claimed him from Montreal in the draft for $30,000.

Tony was neither surprised nor disappointed by the switch. "I knew I wouldn't be with Montreal any longer," he said. "After all, the Canadiens had won the Stanley Cup with those goalies, and their decision to protect them couldn't be faulted. They were established NHL goalies and I wasn't. I had no beefs about not being protected. Besides, all I wanted was a chance to show what I could do in the NHL, and I couldn't see that there was any way I'd get it with Montreal."

So Tony went to Chicago. It was the perfect place for a young goalie who wanted an opportunity to demonstrate his ability. During the 1960s the Black Hawks were the NHL's highest-scoring team. The free-wheeling club featured the league's two top offensive stars, Bobby Hull and Stan Mikita. Although the strong offense provided entertaining hockey for the fans, the team couldn't seem to win a championship. In the 1968–69 season the Hawks had been second-highest scoring team in the NHL, but weak defensive play and erratic goaltending had landed them in the East Division cellar.

The Black Hawks' coach, Billy Reay, changed the club's emphasis for the 1969–70 season. The wide-open, attacking style of hockey gave way to Reay's defense-oriented approach to the game, featuring close checking and sound positional play. Reay was also looking for a top-flight goalie to complete the new defense.

Esposito had to fight Denis DeJordy and Dave Dryden for the Hawks' goaltending job, but his sparkling displays during training camp and the preseason games earned him first-string status. Aided by the club's strong defensive performance, Esposito quickly proved he was an excellent big league goalie.

The Hawks, playing their first season in the West Division, spent most of the season in first place. And Esposito had the league's lowest goals-against average for most of the season. Tony played in 63 of the Hawks' 78 games in 1969–70 and his exceptional 2.17 goals-against average earned him the Vezina Trophy as top goalie and the Calder Trophy as best NHL rookie. He also established a modern-league record for shutouts with 15 to break the record of 13 set in 1953–54 by Harry Lumley of the Toronto Maple Leafs.

Not everyone was intimidated by the big goalie, though. One NHL player who showed he could score goals against Tony Esposito was Phil Esposito. The first time the two brothers faced each other on an NHL rink, the Hawks and

**Playing with the Black Hawks, Tony makes a save on his brother Phil (7), the Boston Bruins' super-scorer.**

Bruins played a 2–2 tie and Phil counted both goals for Boston. Chicago and Boston were long-standing rivals and contenders for the Stanley Cup, hockey's top team prize. Whenever the two teams met, the boys' parents had a problem: which team would they cheer?

"My wife has trouble when the boys' teams play each other and our sons are hot rivals," said their father, Pat Esposito. "One second she's hollering at Phil to shoot the puck, and the next second she's calling him a rat for scoring on his brother. I think I have it a little easier because I enjoy every goal Phil scores and every shot Tony stops. Most fathers would be happy to have one son in the NHL, but I have two of them there."

Mr. Esposito's youngest son was quick to share the credit for his great success. "A goalie's secrets are a little luck and a great deal of help," he explained. "I had plenty of both that year. I was lucky to get fifteen shutouts that season because in several of those games, shots hit the goal posts, which shows that the margin was very narrow. Besides, a shutout to me indicates a strong defensive effort by the entire team, not just a bunch of big saves by the goalie."

In the semi-final round of the 1970 Stanley Cup playoffs, the Hawks met the Boston Bruins, and once more the Esposito brothers were face to face. Phil got a big edge in the family battle, scoring five goals as Boston won four games in a row to eliminate the Black Hawks.

"I helped my brother, too," Tony said. "Phil was in a scoring slump during the season, and we talked on the phone. I told him that he wasn't handling the puck enough and he wasn't shooting enough, either. He thanked me for the advice with all those playoff goals!"

During the next two seasons, Tony demonstrated the consistency which all NHL goalies must have. He played 57 games in 1970–71 and had a 2.27 average. When Chicago's other goalie, Gerry Desjardins, broke his arm late in the season, Esposito played all of the Hawks' 18 playoff contests. His brilliant work carried the team to within a goal of the Stanley Cup, but Chicago lost to Montreal, 3–2, in the seventh game of the finals.

Most teams in the NHL were beginning to use a pair of goalies, rather than ask one to take up the whole burden. In 1971–72 the Black Hawks acquired goalie Gary Smith in a trade, and he and Esposito formed a perfect partnership. They won the Vezina Trophy, and Esposito allowed only 82 goals in 48 games for an amazing 1.76 average. Tony also earned first All-Star team honors and was ranked with Montreal's Ken Dryden as the best goalie in hockey.

Despite his three years of excellence, Esposito's clumsy-looking but extremely effective style was often criticized. Many experts had predicted that Esposito's lack of style would prove to be his downfall. They thought that big league shooters would take advantage of his weak points, especially the fact that he fell to the ice a great deal. It didn't work out that way, though. Esposito's size (5-foot-11, 190 pounds), which allowed him to fill a sizeable portion of the net, his quick reflexes, excellent catching hand and competitive fire more than made up for any technical shortcomings.

"I always had a big laugh when someone knocked Tony's so-called lack of style," Chicago's coach Reay said. "Look at his record! If his style is so poor, how come more goals don't get into our net when he's playing? Tony's strength is that he's very alert. Some goalies are a split-second behind the play—Tony is usually a split-second ahead of it. Sure, he's a bit awkward, but that's only in appearance because he's very seldom out of position."

Esposito appreciated coach Reay's confidence in him. Like many goaltenders, Tony detested the team workouts where he had to defend against heavy shooting from his own teammates.

"I don't put much stock in practice," Tony said. "Playing goal is a strange business, and every goalie has his own approach to it. Billy Reay leaves me alone and permits me to practice when I feel I need it. I don't see anything very brave about playing well in a workout. In fact, if one of our players with a hard shot, like Dennis Hull, shoots a slapper from 30 feet away, I won't even try to stop it. I just get out of the net, and it can go in."

After the 1972 season Esposito was named one of the goalies on Team Canada, the top NHL stars who would meet the Soviet Union's National Team in the first hockey confrontation between the North American professionals and the eleven-time world amateur champions.

At training camp for the series against the Russians, Esposito had no opportunity to study his opponents' play. When asked if the lack of a "book" on the Russian shooters was a handicap to him, he replied: "I don't even keep a book on the NHL shooters. The smart shooters, the guys I really have to worry about, never do the same thing twice in a row, so what good is a book on them? A shot is a shot!"

**Esposito (center) minds Team Canada's net in the historic 1972 "world series" against the Soviet National Team.**

Tony was a standout in the grinding eight-game series. Team Canada won it, four games to three with one game tied. It was a hard-fought battle—the deciding eighth-game goal came just 34 seconds before the game's end. In the four games in which Esposito played, Team Canada had two wins, a tie and a loss.

Tony wasn't the only Esposito who starred against the Russians. Phil, playing on the same side for a change, was the top player on either side with a magnificent display of all-around excellence. Team Canada would not have had its narrow victory without the brothers Esposito.

Off the ice Tony Esposito was just the opposite of his fun-loving, practical-joking brother. Tony frequently wore a sour, serious expression.

"I don't joke around very much because playing goal is how I earn my living, and I don't want to be distracted," he explained. "There's nothing very funny about playing goal. I have trouble with my emotions, and I'm very nervous before a game. My big worry is that I'll make a mistake. If I make a bad move, the puck is in, the red light is on, and thinking about that makes me ill."

Luckily for Tony, it wasn't very often that the red light went on while *he* was minding the net.

# JACQUES PLANTE
## The Innovator

The style of modern professional hockey was shaped by various forces. Over the years, perhaps the greatest influence on the style of play came from a few individual stars who "invented" new ways to play their positions. Soon a style pioneered by one great player was adopted by others and became standard in pro hockey.

For instance, Bobby Hull had a strong influence on offensive play. When the Chicago Black Hawks' mighty winger scored countless goals with his booming slap-shot in the late 1950s, other players quickly made the slap-shot their main weapon.

Defensive play was revolutionized by two Boston Bruin stars. In the 1920s and '30s, Eddie Shore became the first great rushing defenseman. Up to that point, rearguards concentrated almost exclusively on defense. Seldom did they venture beyond their team's blueline. But Shore managed to attack as well as defend. When Bobby Orr joined the Bruins in 1966, he carried the offensive participation which Shore had started and others had expanded to new extremes. Orr even won the National Hockey League scoring championship—an unheard of achievement for a defenseman.

But no single player placed his personal stamp on a position to the extent that Jacques Plante influenced the style and technique of goaltending. During his 18 seasons in the NHL with the Montreal Canadiens, New York Rangers, St. Louis Blues, Toronto Maple Leafs and Boston Bruins, Plante made many innovations which most goalies now take for granted.

Jacques was the first goalie to skate far from his goal crease to trap a loose puck and direct it to a teammate or clear it out of danger. Until Plante ventured into the corners and behind the net, goalies seldom skated more than five feet away from the crease.

Plante said he developed his wandering ways when he was playing junior hockey in Quebec City. "Our four defensemen all had flaws," he explained. "One couldn't skate backwards,

**Jacques Plante, Toronto's wandering goalie, strays behind the net to get between the puck and the Atlanta Flames' Ray Comeau (18).**

one couldn't turn to his left, one couldn't turn to his right and the fourth couldn't pass the puck accurately to our blueline. Somebody had to clear the loose pucks, so I started doing it myself. Because it worked and I felt it helped the team, I continued to do it right up to the NHL."

At first the Montreal management criticized Plante's safaris, fearing he would get trapped out of position and his opponents would have easy shots at the unprotected net. "There were assorted arguments on both sides about the merits of a goalie going out of the net," Jacques said. "But before long, other goalies were doing the same thing."

Plante was also responsible for another NHL first. Strange as it seems now, goalies used to defend against shots traveling at more than 110 miles per hour with their faces unprotected. But that changed when Plante, again with some management opposition, began wearing a face mask in 1959.

Plante had acquired more than 200 stitches in his face from flying pucks and sticks during the maskless portion of his career. He had frequently thought about wearing a mask, but couldn't find one that wouldn't limit his vision. Other goalies in earlier eras had experimented with wire masks similar to those worn by baseball catchers but had found them unsatisfactory.

In the 1958 playoffs Jacques was cut on the forehead by a puck. Bill Burchmore, an employee of Fibreglas Canada who had seen the game, wrote a letter to Plante outlining an idea he had for a lightweight, tight-fitting mask that could be molded to the goalie's face.

"I was interested, but I had doubts about the idea," Plante recalled. "Then, in the summer of 1959, I decided to try it. A plaster cast was made of my face in the hospital by a doctor, and Burchmore used it to shape a mask. I was a pretty frightening sight in that first mask."

When Jacques tried the mask in preseason games, he encountered a great deal of opposition. Many coaches claimed a mask indicated that a goaltender was losing his nerve. And Montreal coach Toe Blake was afraid the mask would cause Plante to lose sight of the puck at his feet.

"Blake told me that if I had a bad night wearing the mask, the fans would blame it and get on me," Plante said. "I think he also saw it as a sign that I was puck-shy."

So Jacques finally gave up the idea. But on November 1, 1959, he was struck on the side of his nose by a shot in a game at New York. It took seven stitches to close the deep cut. Because NHL teams used only one goalie at that time, Plante had to return to the net. But that time he wore his mask. When the Canadiens and their masked goalie won the next eleven games, Plante's bare-faced days were over.

Although other goalies were slow to adopt the mask, Terry Sawchuk, the great netminder of the Detroit Red Wings, started to wear one in 1962. Other goalies eventually tried the masks, and by the 1970s only Gump Worsley of the Minnesota North Stars and Joe Daley of the World Hockey Association's Winnipeg Jets were playing major league hockey without facial protection.

In 1970 Jacques went into a partnership with a plastics expert and an engineer to open a plant that manufactured goalie masks. Two years later they were producing 25,000 masks annually for goalies at all levels and age groups in hockey.

Plante's revolutionary contributions to hockey came as no surprise to those who knew him. He was regarded as one of the great students of the game, the possessor of a keen intelligence and the analytical mind to learn every fine point of the sport. He was acknowledged as the master by other goalies, who frequently sought his advice when they were having problems. Most netminders admitted that they studied his technique closely.

"Plante had a truly remarkable mind," said Maple Leaf coach John McLellan. "Not only did he know everything about his own position, but he made a study of every aspect of the game and passed along advice to players in all positions. When he joined our team in 1970, it was the greatest thing that ever happened to me. He didn't second-guess me. In fact, I asked for his help. I told him to tell me about it if he noticed anything."

Plante claimed his knowledge of playing goal was self-taught and he merely took a professional approach to his job. "For me to be the best possible goalie, I had to learn as much about the game as I could," he explained. "And not just about my own position but the complete game of hockey. No detail in anyone's job is too small to be overlooked.

"Nobody ever taught me the way to play goal. I was never coached at the position. The skill I developed was learned from personal experience and from studying the mistakes made by other goalies. Of course, hockey is a physical game, and maintaining the best conditioning is important. But playing goal is really a very scientific thing, and that's the approach I tried to take."

Plante was as unique off the ice as he was on it. During his years in Toronto near the end of his career, he lived alone in a rented apartment while his wife and their two sons remained at the family home in suburban Montreal. Jacques was a loner who followed an almost rigid schedule. He went to bed every night at 9:30, cooked all his own meals and spent much of his time away from the rink answering the hundreds of letters he received each week from fans. Boys who asked for goaltending advice received a sheet which listed 15 of Plante's goalie tips.

An avid reader, Jacques disliked novels and concentrated on biographies of such diverse personalities as Winston Churchill and Jacqueline Kennedy. While watching television, he attached weights to his feet and lifted his legs to strengthen his knees. He even knit his own undershirts when he couldn't find the kind he wanted in the stores. He was also a competent landscape painter, was once a partner in a Montreal hair-dressing salon and was much in demand as a commentator on hockey telecasts.

But of course his greatest talent was his goaltending. The record book supplied the best testimony to Plante's abilities. Seven times he won the Vezina Trophy as the NHL's leading goalie, and seven times he was named to the All-Star team. Through 1971–72 his goals-against average for 797 NHL contests was 2.38 per game, the best of all the great goalies, and he had 79 career shutouts. In the Stanley Cup playoffs Plante had a 2.09 average for 110 games. When *The Hockey News*, the sport's top publication, celebrated its 25th anniversary in 1971, its writers picked a quarter-century all-star team. Plante was named as the goalie.

The oldest of eleven children, Jacques was born in 1929 in a farmhouse near Mont Carmel, Quebec. The family later moved to Shawinigan Falls, where his father worked as a machinist.

"You could say I grew up in poverty, because we didn't have very much," Plante said. "As the oldest in a large family, I had to help out around home—washing, scrubbing floors and cooking. My mother taught me to knit, and eventually I could knit a pair of socks in three hours.

"I never wore shoes in the summer except to go to church, and the only time we had soft drinks in the house was as a special treat at Christmas. I drank champagne from the Stanley Cup six times, and it never tasted as good as those Christmas soft drinks at home."

Plante began his hockey career as a six-year-old defenseman on the frozen ponds and rivers of Canada. However, a chronic asthma condition, which bothered him as long as he played the game, forced him to play goal.

"In sub-zero weather I had difficulty breathing when I skated hard because of the asthma," Plante recalled. "I was able to play goal, though, with no trouble. If it hadn't been for my asthma, I probably would have stayed on defense and never progressed beyond pond hockey."

When Jacques was twelve, he earned the goaltending job on his school's hockey team, which was made up of boys in their late teens. He had been watching the team practice one day when the regular goalie got into an argument with the coach and quit. Plante volunteered to replace him, and the job was his for the rest of the season. Two years later, he was playing goal for teams in four different leagues at the midget, juvenile, junior and intermediate levels.

Plante's ability quickly attracted the attention of hockey scouts. When he was eighteen he moved to Quebec City where he became a junior hockey star with the Quebec Citadels. He expressed his individuality there by wandering far from the net to aid his leaky defense. His uniform for those games included a wool cap (a toque) which he had knitted himself.

"Some of the rinks were cold so I wore the toque to keep my head warm," he said. "Some people called me a 'showboat,' but there were good reasons for the things I did."

Plante joined the Montreal Royals, a senior amateur team, in 1949 and was a practice goalie for the NHL Canadiens. His outstanding play in the Quebec Senior Hockey League made him a splendid professional prospect, and several NHL teams attempted to make a trade with the Canadiens for his services.

During his second season with the Royals, Jacques made his NHL debut with the Canadiens when Montreal's top goalie, Gerry McNeil, was injured. Plante replaced him for a game against the New York Rangers. The Canadiens' coach, Dick Irvin, refused to allow Plante to wear his toque. But even without it he played effectively in his first big league game, which the Canadiens won 4–1. Plante played two more games, a win and a tie, before McNeil returned. In those three games he yielded only four goals.

Plante signed his first pro contract in January 1953 and was assigned to the American Hockey League's Buffalo Bisons, where he performed brilliantly for the last-place team. Then McNeil's nerves gave out when the Canadiens were involved in a hectic playoff series against the Chicago Black Hawks, and Plante returned to Montreal. He contributed a variety of dazzling saves to a Canadiens' 3–0 victory in his first playoff game. Plante was in goal for four games as Montreal eliminated Chicago and the Boston Bruins to win the Cup. He allowed the opposition only seven goals and was in the net when Montreal clinched the championship with a 1–0 overtime victory.

By the next season McNeil had recovered, and Plante returned to Buffalo, becoming the AHL's leading goalie. Late in the schedule he was called up from Buffalo when McNeil was injured again. This time, Plante had arrived to stay. He played 17 NHL games, surrendered only 27 goals and earned five shutouts.

That was the start of Plante's nine distinguished seasons with the Canadiens, who had built up what many experts considered the greatest team in NHL history. The Canadiens won the Stanley Cup five consecutive times between 1956 and 1960, and Plante was the leading goalie each of those seasons. During that period the team featured a glittering array of NHL stars—Plante in goal, Doug Harvey and Tom Johnson on defense, Maurice and Henri Richard, Jean Beliveau, Boom-Boom Geoffrion and Dickie Moore on offense.

Although Plante was dominant among NHL goalies, life wasn't always easy for him. The rabid fans at the Montreal Forum never really appreciated Jacques, and they were convinced that he skated after loose pucks merely to gain attention.

The relationship between Plante and the Canadiens' coach Toe Blake wasn't very smooth either. Blake not only disapproved of Plante's wanderlust, but he also thought that Plante's assorted ailments and asthma attacks were all in his mind.

**Plante guards the Montreal net during the 1955 Stanley Cup playoffs.**

One season Plante complained of a sore knee, and although x-rays showed no damage, he had surgery during the offseason. "The doctors removed three pieces of cartilage," Plante recalled. "Only then did people believe the knee really was injured. They figured I'd been faking it."

The Canadiens sagged slightly in the early 1960s after several top stars retired or were traded. In 1961–62 Plante won his sixth Vezina Trophy and earned the Hart Trophy as the NHL's most valuable player. However, just one year later the Canadiens traded Plante to the New York Rangers in a multi-player deal that brought goalie Gump Worsley to Montreal. Controversy about the trade raged for months in Montreal, where Jacques' supporters claimed that he had been made the scapegoat for Montreal's skid to third place.

The Canadiens' managing director, Frank Selke, denied that charge. "We couldn't depend on Plante any more because of his health problems," he said. "Toe Blake couldn't have taken much more without punching Plante in the mouth. Jacques was probably the best goalie I'd ever seen, but that didn't mean he could run the hockey team."

The New York fans gave Plante a rousing welcome when he appeared in a Ranger uniform. He had a respectable 3.38 average with the defensively weak Rangers, but even his excellent goaltending wasn't enough to lift the mediocre

New York team into the playoffs.

Plante was unhappy in New York because his wife and family had remained in Montreal, and his life was lonely in the strange city. In the 1964–65 season the Rangers twice demoted Plante to their Baltimore farm team in the American League, which made him even more unhappy. To top it all off, his wife was very ill, and the doctors told Plante that she was on the verge of a nervous breakdown. So at the end of the season the 36-year-old goalie retired from the NHL.

Plante spent three years out of hockey, although he was never far away from his sport. He worked as a promotional representative for a Montreal brewery, wrote a hockey column for a Montreal French-language newspaper, made many appearances as a television commentator and was president of the Quebec Junior Hockey League. He played hockey in charity games with the Montreal NHL Oldtimers, and during the summer he worked out with a lacrosse team to keep in shape.

In December 1965, Plante was recruited as a special goalie for the Montreal Junior Canadiens in a game against the Soviet Union's National Team, which was on a successful Canadian tour. Plante's superior display produced a 2–1 win for the Canadian team.

It was a big shock to everyone when the St. Louis Blues claimed the 40-year old Plante from

New York in the 1968 intra-league draft. The Blues planned to team him in goal with 37-year-old Glenn Hall. It was an even bigger shock that Jacques agreed to come out of retirement.

"My wife had regained her health completely, and she told me that if I'd like to go back to hockey, it was fine with her," Jacques said. "I appreciated the three years away from the game. I was relaxed and confident that I could play again. I'd maintained good conditioning, and the St. Louis offer was a good one.

"I was a little worried about my left knee, which had given me much trouble in my last year with the Rangers. I told the St. Louis management about it, and they had me examined by a doctor. I had surgery in July, and some torn cartilage was removed. When training camp started, I quickly found out that I hadn't lost my reflexes or my love of the game."

Plante and Hall supplied the Blues with the best goaltending in the NHL during 1968–69. They shared the Vezina Trophy for the best goals-against average. In an amazing comeback, Plante built a 1.96 average in 37 games and had five shutouts. In ten playoff games he allowed only 14 goals. The following season Plante's average was 2.19 for 32 games.

"I don't think I ever played better than I did in St. Louis," Plante said enthusiastically. "The atmosphere with the Blues was very relaxed, the fans in St. Louis were great and Glenn Hall and I

**Playing for the St. Louis Blues, Plante knocks away a shot by Montreal's Jean Beliveau. Puck is at lower left.**

got along tremendously well. I thoroughly enjoyed it."

Plante, then 41, changed teams again in 1970 when St. Louis sold him to the Toronto Maple Leafs. Once more, some hockey experts questioned the wisdom of an NHL team acquiring an ancient goalie, and once again Plante showed that he was still in the front rank of NHL puck-stoppers.

Operating behind a young defense, which improved immensely with his help, Plante had a 1.88 goals-against average in 40 games. In 1971–72, as the Leafs floundered through a mediocre season, his mark was 2.62.

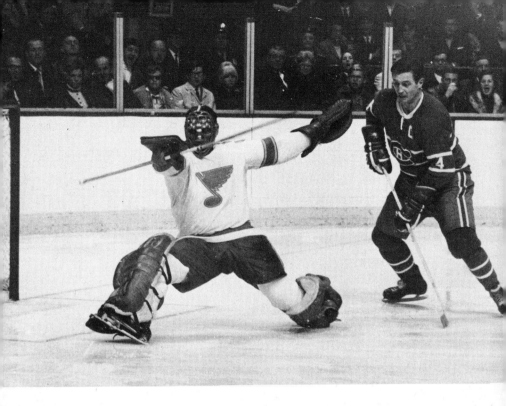

Early in the 1972–73 season a broken finger sidelined Plante briefly, but his play showed no deterioration. Hard work in practice sessions and offseason tennis workouts maintained his amazing physical condition.

Late in the 1972–73 season Plante was traded by the Maple Leafs to the Bruins, a team plagued by weak goaltending. When Plante arrived in Boston the Bruins were in third place in the East Division, five points behind the New York Rangers. Plante played in eight of the team's 14 remaining games, and the Bruins won seven as they moved up to second place. Plante allowed only 16 goals in his eight contests, but in the first round of the Stanley Cup playoffs the Bruins were eliminated by the Rangers in five games.

Plante was asked how long he figured his remarkable career could continue.

"I play one game at a time, and one year at a time," the 44-year-old goalie replied. "So long as I enjoy it and so long as they want me, I'll go on."

# JOHNNY BOWER
## The Reluctant Goalie

There's no doubt about it: in the world of hockey, the National Hockey League is definitely the big time. Youngsters skating on frozen lakes and rivers dream of graduating to NHL stardom. Junior and senior amateurs and American Hockey League professionals often play for years, hoping to be scouted by the top teams. It sometimes seems that just about everyone who owns a shinny stick is waiting for the chance to prove himself in the big league.

But Johnny Bower was an exception to that rule. In 1958, Bower was playing goal for the American Hockey League's Cleveland Barons when he got a chance to play for the NHL's Toronto Maple Leafs—and he almost turned it down. What made his reluctance especially hard to understand was the fact that Bower was 33 years old at the time, an age when most hockey players were considered to be near the end of their careers. If the aging goalie rejected the Leafs' offer, it was unlikely that he would ever get another chance.

Toronto's invitation was not the first Bower had received to play in the NHL. In fact, the 13-year veteran of professional hockey had already had one discouraging season (1953–54) in the league with the New York Rangers.

Bower later explained why he hesitated to leave the Barons. "At that time, Cleveland was the best place to play outside of the NHL," he said. "I was very happy there, and my family liked it. I'd had my try at the NHL, which wasn't too happy, and really, I didn't think I could be much help to Toronto."

With the help of a good two-year contract, the Leafs finally persuaded Bower to take another chance with the NHL. So Johnny moved into the Toronto net—and stayed there for twelve seasons, playing a key role in the Leafs' four Stanley Cup victories in the 1960s. He won the Vezina Trophy twice and was named twice to the first All-Star team.

One of his greatest NHL achievements came in the 1967 playoffs when Bower was 42. Johnny

and another oldtimer, 38-year-old Terry Sawchuk, were the Leaf goalies during a hot-and-
cold season when Toronto finished a weak third
in the final standings. Both goalies had battled
injuries all year. Back and shoulder problems and
some dislocated and broken fingers had limited
Bower's action to 24 games during the regular
schedule.

In the Stanley Cup playoffs, however, Bower
and Sawchuk managed to supply some of the
finest goaltending ever seen in postseason play,
as the Leafs eliminated the Chicago Black
Hawks and the Montreal Canadiens to win the
Cup.

The Leaf manager-coach Punch Imlach
called his team "The Old Folks' Home" because
the roster contained seven players who were 36
years of age or older. "Most people said I was
crazy to stick with those old guys for as long as I
did," said the happy coach after the playoffs.
"But they forgot that Bower and Sawchuk
weren't any ordinary old guys. Of course, playing
goal is a very strenuous job which requires good
physical conditioning. But it also demands wisdom, experience and the ability to handle pressure, and my old goalies certainly had that.

"I've always said that Bower is the most
amazing athlete in the world, and I don't think
there's much argument about it. Playing goal is
the toughest job in sports, and Bower was able to
do it better than anyone else when he was well

past his fortieth birthday. If that doesn't make him the most amazing athlete, then I'd like to know what does."

Some people suspected that Bower was even older than his listed age. The NHL record book stated that he was born on November 8, 1924, at Prince Albert, Saskatchewan, but no birth certificate was ever found. Members of his own family weren't even sure that 1924 was the correct year of Johnny's birth.

Bower himself frequently gave varying birthdates, perhaps to get even with all those who needled him about his age. "I've lied about my age so often that I can't remember how old I really am," he joked.

Bower had seen overseas duty with the Canadian Army in World War II, but claimed he had lied about his age to enlist when he was only 16, two years under the legal minimum. Once when Bower mentioned something that had happened to him in "the world war," a young Leaf replied: "Which one, Johnny? World War One or World War Two?"

Bower never discouraged the speculation about his age. In fact, he seemed to enjoy it. His teammates, especially the younger ones, kidded Bower repeatedly, calling him "Gramps" or "the old man."

To the NHL shooters, Bower's age didn't really mean much. They soon discovered that he was among the finest NHL goalies in history,

**Bower finds the net a little crowded when a Toronto teammate drops in.**

with a complete bag of netminder's tricks plus a mastery of all the skills of his trade.

Bower had size (5-foot-11, 190 pounds) and great competitive desire (he hated to surrender goals, even in workouts). Most hockey experts agreed that he was without equal in the art of goaltending, positioning himself so well that the

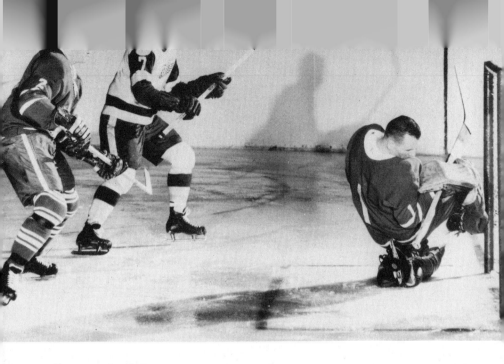

**Bower gets a skate on the puck to save an almost sure goal by Detroit's Norm Ullman in the 1963 Stanley Cup playoffs.**

net openings for the opposing shooters were almost nonexistent.

Bower was the master of the goalie's "poke-check." When an attacker approached his net with the puck, Bower would slowly glide out to meet him. By "playing the angles," keeping himself between the puck and the open net, Bower usually forced the attacker to attempt a deke (or fake) rather than a shot. Then when the player tried to move the puck from one side to the other and pull it around the goalie, Bower's big stick would flick out and knock the puck away—often knocking the skates out from under the shooter in the process.

46

Another of Bower's strengths was his ability to use his legs to stop shots headed for the low corners of the net, the most difficult save for a goalie to make. He was extraordinarily fast at "doing the splits," kicking out his pads to knock the puck away.

In a Stanley Cup game against the Canadiens, Bower was caught out of position at the side of the net by a pass which gave Montreal's Dick Duff the entire net as a target. Duff drove a quick shot toward the low corner away from Bower—a sure goal—but the big goalie did the splits to halt the puck for an incredible save.

After the game, the Canadiens' great center Jean Beliveau was asked if he thought anyone else could have stopped the shot. "I don't think so," he said. "In fact, I doubt if any other goalie would have even tried to stop it."

When he was a boy in the small city of Prince Albert, Bower became a goalie because his family couldn't afford to buy skates for him. The boys of the town played on the frozen North Saskatchewan river, and goal was the one position young Johnny could play in his shoes.

"Kids today just can't understand it, but we had no money for hockey equipment," Bower explained. "My father worked in a meat-packing plant, and his money went for the necessities. My first hockey sticks were the true 'shinny' variety. My father would cut a branch with the proper bend off a jackpine or black poplar tree, and I'd shave it down to make a hockey stick.

"One of the neighborhood kids named Eddie Helko was really smart. He made a pair of goal pads from an old mattress. He cut them out and sewed them up at the sides. He used rings cut from an old rubber inner tube to hold them on his legs. We made a little rink in his backyard and took turns shooting at each other. Eddie would wear the pads until I scored five goals on him, then I'd wear them until he scored five."

Bower's first hockey hero was Don Deacon, a player with the Prince Albert Mintos, a senior team. By carrying Deacon's skates Bower earned his way into the rink whenever the Mintos played. One day Deacon called his ten-year-old fan into the dressing room and gave him a pair of battered old skates.

"They were the wrong size, too big for me," Bower recalled. "But I worshipped those skates even though I couldn't get used to them."

Bower tended goal for various boys' teams in Prince Albert, then interrupted his hockey career to serve in the Canadian Army. When he received a medical discharge in 1943, Bower joined the Prince Albert junior team.

It was doubtful that the army veteran was really eligible for junior hockey, which had an age limit of 20 years. But since Bower's birth certificate could not be found in the official records, he was allowed to finish the 1943–44 season.

Bower turned professional in the 1945–46 season and began an exceptional eight-year stint with the Cleveland Barons. He consistently was the best goalie in the AHL, maintaining an excellent goals-against average in a league where offense was stressed. But despite his success, Bower remained in the minors. Only six big league goalie jobs existed in those days—there were only six NHL teams and each carried just one netminder on its roster—so major league positions were hard to come by.

"I never worried much about not getting a shot at the NHL," Bower said. "I was making a good living in Cleveland, and I was happy there."

After eight years with Cleveland Bower did attend the New York Rangers' training camp in the fall of 1953. But there seemed to be no way he could earn a spot with the NHL team. Goalie Gump Worsley had won the Calder Trophy as the NHL's best rookie the previous season, so he had the inside track for the Ranger goaling job.

However, Bower's excellent play in training camp and the preseason games made a tremendous impression on the New York management. When the season opened, the 29-year-old Bower was the Rangers' first-string goalie and Worsley was dispatched to the Vancouver Canucks of the Western League.

Bower showed he could perform strongly in the NHL, earning a goals-against average of 2.60 in 70 games for the fifth-place Rangers. But

Bower's first try at the NHL lasted just one season. The following year Bower and Worsley traded places. Worsley regained the Ranger job, and Bower was assigned to Vancouver. Then in 1955–56, Bower was sent to the Providence Reds of the AHL, where he spent the next two seasons.

In 1957–58 he was reassigned to Cleveland, where he became the AHL's leading goalie (with a 2.19 average) and most valuable player. Bower was prepared to spend his remaining pro years with the Barons.

But a surprising turn of events in Toronto changed all that. In the 1957–58 season, for the first time in their history, the Leafs finished in last place. Goaltending was the team's weak point. Leaf coach Billy Reay scouted the minor pro leagues for a new netminder and decided that Bower was the best available man even though he was already 33 years old.

Early in the 1958–59 season Coach Reay was fired by Leaf manager Punch Imlach, who became Toronto's manager-coach. Thus began the highly successful relationship between the fiery, unpredictable Imlach and the easy-going new goalie, Johnny Bower.

Imlach was in the middle of a rebuilding miracle when Bower arrived in Toronto. The Leaf farm system had supplied a splendid array of young talent, and Imlach was filling the gaps with older players who were thought to be over

**Charging out of the Toronto net, Johnny throws a Montreal player head over heels to make a spectacular save in the 1959 playoffs.**

the hill by other NHL teams.

"There was a great deal of joking about Punch and his old folks home, but he knew exactly what he was doing when he picked up all the older players," Bower said. "He had a big crop of young players with little NHL experience, and the older guys helped them, especially in the tight-checking style Imlach's teams used."

The new, improved Leafs earned a playoff spot on the final day of the 1958–59 season. Bower's goaltending was a major factor in the club's late surge. In the playoffs, again with Bower in a key role, the underdog Leafs eliminated the Boston Bruins in the semi-finals and gave the power-house Montreal Canadiens some tough opposition before losing in the final.

The Leafs' steady climb to a contending position continued as Bower quickly established himself as a top NHL goalie. During the 1960–61 season he won the Vezina Trophy with a 2.50 average and earned first All-Star team honors.

The Leafs had matured into one of hockey's best teams by 1961–62, when they won the first of three consecutive Stanley Cups. The most important ingredient in those victories was the amazing goaltending of Bower. In the Leafs' three Cup-winning years, he maintained playoff averages of 2.20, 1.60 and 2.14.

"I played against all the great goalies," said Dave Keon, the Leafs' fine center. "But if my team had to win a big game, then Bower would be the only goalie I'd want in our net. He was a great goalie all the time, but in the big games, the ones that really meant something, like the playoffs, he was the best."

As he reached and then passed his 40th birthday, Bower continued to excel in his demanding position. The Leafs slipped from their place of prominence after the 1964 Stanley Cup victory, but in 1967 they rallied for a surprise title with the help of "old folks" Bower and Terry Sawchuk in goal.

During the 1969–70 season Bower passed his 45th birthday, the age at which NHL players are eligible to receive their pension payments. Thus, another milestone was added to the Bower saga, and Johnny became the first professional athlete to qualify for his pension while still an active performer.

Bower's continuing ability to play at an age when most athletes were long retired had a simple explanation: He was the hardest worker on the team. In practice sessions he drove himself to exhaustion, skating full-tilt while wearing 35 pounds of goalie equipment.

"The only way I know how to play this game is through hard work," he said. "Besides, nothing ever seemed to come to me in this world unless I worked for it."

Although all but two of his teeth had been knocked out by sticks and pucks and he had sustained close to 300 stitches on his face, Bower refused to wear a face mask when most goalies began using the protection in the 1960s.

"I gave the mask a tryout in practice once, and the first time someone took a shot at me, I ducked," he explained. "I'd never done that before without a mask, so I threw it away and never tried one again.

"A mask would be okay if you wore it from the time you started to play hockey. After all, it protects your head and that's where your brains are supposed to be. But then, being a goalie makes it questionable if you have any brains."

There was no doubt that Bower had more

than enough brains. A warm, immensely likable man, he was one of the most popular players ever to wear a Maple Leaf sweater and one of Canada's best-loved sports personalities. When he finally retired from the net in 1970, Bower joined the Maple Leaf scouting staff and offered expert advice to the young goalies in the team's chain.

Despite his initial reluctance about joining the league, Johnny Bower became one of the NHL's most enthusiastic supporters. Asked to describe the biggest thrill in his long hockey career, the 46-year-old goalie replied: "Just winning a job in the NHL. I never expected to stick when I was 33 years old."

# GLENN HALL
## "Mr. Goalie"

"Playing goal was a winter of misery for me," said Glenn Hall, looking back on his NHL career. "I sometimes asked myself what the hell I was doing there. Plenty of times I was tempted to get into my car and head for home. By the end of the season, I was tired out and fed up with everything. It took me to July to recover completely from a season."

The tensions of playing goal in the National Hockey League wore down many of the men who chose the job as their profession. Several goalies went into early retirement when their nerves rebelled at the constant pressure-cooker atmosphere in which they were forced to perform.

No goalie ever showed the effects of this pressure as much as Glenn Hall did. He often claimed he hated his job, yet he stuck with it, playing 16 seasons with the Detroit Red Wings, Chicago Black Hawks and St. Louis Blues. And his performance on the ice was not merely good, it was great. Long before he finally retired, Glenn Hall was known to fans as "Mr. Goalie."

Jacques Plante, who was Glenn's goaltending partner for two very successful seasons in St. Louis, said he was amazed to discover just how much Hall was affected by the pressures of the job.

"His face would be drawn and tight, and Glenn often was sick to his stomach before a game," Plante recalled. "Sometimes he was sick between periods. It was very surprising that he could endure all that and still be one of the very best goalies who ever played the position. I think the challenge of the job kept him going. There was no way it was going to get the best of him."

The stress and strain never changed Hall's performances on the ice, however. Despite all the physical and psychological pain he suffered, Hall somehow managed to rack up an incredible streak of consecutive games played—502 between 1955 and 1963.

"Few people realized just what an accomplishment that was," Plante said. "For Glenn to carry the load of tending goal in the NHL for that long with no breaks was really amazing."

The record book supplied further testimony to Hall's greatness. From the time he joined Detroit in 1955 until his retirement from the St. Louis net in 1971, Hall played in 906 NHL games and maintained a 2.51 goals-against average. During that period he had 84 shutouts. Hall won the Vezina Trophy as leading goalie three times and was chosen for the All-Star team eleven times (including seven first-team nominations).

Hall's style of playing goal was somewhat unconventional. He perfected the "Y" approach to the position. Spreading his legs well apart, he made his body resemble an inverted Y and dug the toes of his skates into the ice. Thus, he made himself as large as possible in front of the net to guard against deflections and screen shots.

"The coaches never liked my style very much," Hall admitted. "But I figured I could cover more of the net that way. With my toes dug in, I was able to move in either direction much more quickly than if I stood straight up."

Hall also fell to the ice more frequently than most top goalies, but his extraordinary reflexes—especially his lightning-fast catching hand—more than made up for that. "There's nothing wrong with falling to the ice if you do it with a purpose in mind," he insisted.

Hall went his own way off the ice as well as on it. He was a loner, and many people called him surly and unpleasant—a reputation he never denied. On road trips he rarely went to the movies or socialized with his teammates, preferring to sit alone in his room. He didn't read books or watch television because he felt it would hurt his eyes. He seldom read newspapers because he claimed the sportswriters knew little about the game, and their reports made him angry. Hall even thought that the fans who asked for autographs were a nuisance.

"I liked it best when nobody recognized me," he said. "Before a game, I kept to myself because I was so miserable I didn't think anyone would want me around. I didn't especially like people, and I couldn't force myself to be a nice guy when I didn't want to be."

Glenn was never happy playing in the big cities. He was raised on a farm and enjoyed the quiet country life and wide open spaces. He detested the crowds, noise and traffic of the cities. During the summers Hall lived on a farm near Edmonton, Alberta, where he said he unwound after the season by walking through the fields by himself.

Hall often talked about retiring from hockey. When he showed up late for Chicago's training camp in 1966, Glenn claimed it was because he'd had to paint the barn on his farm. But there was no barn on Hall's farm. What he had really been doing was looking for a job outside of hockey. When he had no luck finding something suitable, Hall finally reported to training camp.

Glenn Hall was born in 1931 in Humboldt, Saskatchewan, a western Canada railway center. His father was an engineer for the Canadian National Railway. Glenn first learned to play hockey on rugged outdoor rinks, where the boys of the town went every chance they got—even when the temperature dropped to 40 degrees below zero.

As a teenager, Hall played goal for the Humboldt Indians' junior team. It was there that he was discovered in 1949 by Fred Pinkney, the western Canada scout for the Detroit Red Wings. The Wings moved Hall to their junior farm team at Windsor in the fast Ontario Junior A league. Glenn got off to a good start there, and in the 1950–51 season he won the Red Tillson Trophy as the league's most valuable player.

For the next four years Hall played with Detroit's minor professional farm teams at Indianapolis and Edmonton. Although his fine performances stamped him as an outstanding NHL prospect, for a while it seemed he'd never reach the big league. The Wings already had a young and brilliant goalie in Terry Sawchuk and had no use for another netminder. Hall did get a chance to prove he was capable of big-league excellence by twice filling in for Sawchuk when the Wing star was injured. In his eight NHL games as a substitute, Hall yielded only twelve goals.

An opening on the Detroit roster for Hall

appeared suddenly when Red Wing manager Jack Adams traded Sawchuk to the Boston Bruins in 1955. Hall took advantage of his lucky break and had a fantastic rookie season. He played in all 70 games in 1955–56, compiled a 2.11 goals-against average and had twelve shutouts to win the Calder Trophy as best freshman player.

The next year Hall had a goals-against average of 2.24 and was named to the first All-Star team. But a mediocre performance in the 1957 playoffs ended his days with Detroit. The Bruins eliminated the Red Wings in five games, and Glenn yielded 15 goals. Although Hall had played well throughout the regular season, he was not a great "clutch" goalie. When the Wings got an op-

**Red Wing rookie Glenn Hall hits the ice after blocking a shot by New York Ranger Dean Prentice (dark shirt) in a 1955 game.**

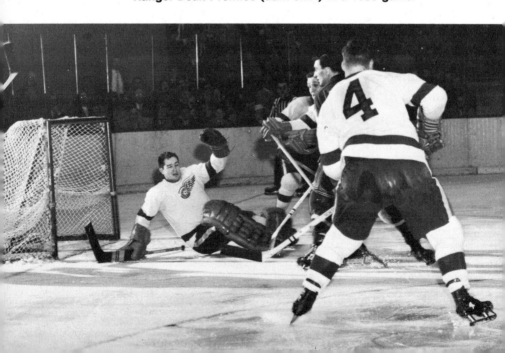

portunity to reacquire Sawchuk from Boston, they traded Hall and their great winger Ted Lindsay to the Chicago Black Hawks for four journeyman players.

Hall was surprised and disappointed by the move. His friends claimed that the sudden trade changed Hall from a talkative, relaxed man into a moody loner. Glenn felt that he alone had been made the scapegoat for a loss which might more justly have been blamed on the whole aging team.

When Glenn moved to Chicago he was determined to show the Red Wings that they had made a big mistake in trading him. The Hawks had spent many years at the bottom of the NHL standings, but when Hall joined them they were rebuilding. Glenn Hall became the key figure in that reconstruction. The rowdy Chicago Stadium fans quickly made Hall a big favorite and nicknamed him "Mr. Goalie."

In his first five seasons in Chicago, Hall played every minute of every game. The productive Hawk farm system and some good deals gradually turned Chicago into a contending team, led by star forwards Bobby Hull and Stan Mikita and defensemen Pierre Pilote and Elmer Vasko. The Hawks were a free-wheeling offensive team, giving their goalie far less defensive support than other teams, so Glenn's low goals-against averages were particularly impressive.

With Hall in the net, the Black Hawks climbed steadily up the NHL ladder. Their progress was capped by a Stanley Cup victory in the 1960–61 season. In the semi-final the Hawks defeated the great Montreal Canadiens who had won the Cup five years in a row. Hall's goaltending was the most important ingredient in that win. He allowed just 27 goals in twelve playoff games, and in one stretch of 135 minutes he completely blanked the powerhouse Canadiens.

The Hawks became hockey's most exciting team with a succession of strong seasons in the 1960s, but were unable to repeat that Stanley Cup victory. Because the Hawks were attack-oriented, Hall always faced a high number of shots on goal. Nevertheless, he maintained an excellent average. He earned first All-Star team honors in three of the four seasons from 1963 to 1966.

Late in the 1960s the two-goalie system was initiated, and Hall's life became a bit easier. Up to that point, NHL teams carried only one goalie, and he had to play in every game. However, when the league expanded in 1967 increased travel and the introduction of a 78-game schedule made the load too heavy for one goalie to carry.

The Hawks were one of the first teams to use two goalies. In the 1966–67 season, Hall and young Denis DeJordy combined to win the Vezina Trophy with the best goals-against average.

"I liked the two-goalie system," Hall said. "Playing in every game, and especially those back-to-back games most weekends, wore a goalie down. With two goalies, I had some time to recover from the bruises of a tough game before I had to play again."

Because of Hall's age (36) and his frequent talk of retirement, the Black Hawks decided to protect their young goalies, DeJordy and Dave Dryden, for the 1967 draft which would stock the six new expansion clubs. The St. Louis Blues, one of the new teams, claimed Hall and signed him to a $47,000 per season contract—the highest ever for a goalie.

Hall shared St. Louis' goaltending chores with Seth Martin, a veteran Canadian amateur goalie, and had a 2.48 average in 48 games during the Blues' first season. But in the midst of his success, Hall again began to think of retiring.

"Glenn told me that his eyesight was deteriorating and that he had no confidence," said St. Louis manager-coach Scotty Bowman. "We had his eyes examined by two doctors who said his sight was 100 percent. Glenn was such a worrier that I don't think he believed them. He said that the one doctor was a young guy who probably hadn't examined very many eyes."

The Blues started their first NHL season very slowly but gradually gained the momentum

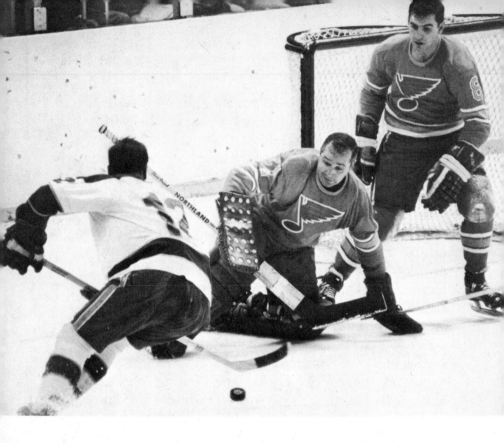

**Hall falls to his knees to block a shot by Minnesota's Wayne Connelly in the 1968 Stanley Cup playoffs.**

to finish in third place in the new West Division. With the help of Hall's brilliant defense, St. Louis eliminated the Philadelphia Flyers and the Minnesota North Stars in the playoffs to qualify for the Stanley Cup final. After just one season in the big league, the newcomers would face the perennial Cup contenders—the mighty Montreal Canadiens.

The experts predicted that Montreal would have a ridiculously easy time against St. Louis' collection of castoff players. Montreal did sweep the series, but the Canadiens had no easy time with Glenn Hall. He played some of the finest goal in the game's history as the Blues made the Canadiens really work for their four wins. No Montreal margin was more than one goal, and two of the games had to go into overtime before a winner could be decided.

Despite the Blues' defeat, Hall was the unanimous choice for the Conn Smythe Trophy as the most valuable player in the playoffs. The Canadiens' Dick Duff was extremely impressed with Hall's performance. "There were many times in that series when we wondered if we'd ever beat that guy," he said.

In 1968–69, Hall got a new goaltending partner when the Blues talked Jacques Plante out of a three-year retirement and drafted him. Plante was 39 at the time and Hall 37, but the two veterans supplied the Blues with superior goaling, combining for a 2.07 average and 13 shutouts to share the Vezina Trophy. Hall had a 2.17 average and eight shutouts in 41 games.

"It was a great arrangement because Jacques was one of the best goalies in history, maybe the best," Hall said. "I played half the games and was able to stay sharp because I didn't get tired."

Hall played two more seasons with St. Louis, and the Blues became the most successful of the expansion clubs. In 1970–71, Hall had a 2.41 average in 32 games. But that year Hall again started to speak of leaving hockey—and it looked as if he actually meant it. After 16 years as a pro, Hall finally retired to his beloved farm in Alberta.

But even that didn't end the story of Hall and hockey. In 1972–73 the veteran netminder returned to the sport as assistant coach of the World Hockey Association's Alberta Oilers. His main duty there was to instruct the team's young goalies. "I like the job," Hall said early in the season. "At least, I don't have to dodge slap-shots."

There was something else Glenn liked about his new job. The Oilers were based in Edmonton, just a short drive from Hall's farm. One of the first things Glenn did with his new-found time and energy was to build a barn on the property—and this time he really did get to paint it.

His reputation as an all-time great goalie secure, Glenn Hall was home again.

# KEN DRYDEN
## A Man for All Seasons

A hockey executive once commented that goalies were "different," a breed apart from the other men who played the game. Most likely, Ken Dryden was one of the men he had in mind. Even among the unusual collection of men who pursued the exotic profession of goaltending, Dryden stood out as a unique individual. He was a man like no other in hockey.

The path that Dryden traveled to reach the front rank of NHL goalies was as unusual as the man himself. First he decided not to play Junior A hockey in the Canadian leagues, where most professional players were developed. Instead, he accepted a hockey scholarship at Cornell University. Following a distinguished All-America college hockey career, he turned down a pro contract offer from the Montreal Canadiens to join the Canadian National Team—and to begin studying for a law degree.

Dryden finally turned pro and joined the Canadiens' American Hockey League farm team, the Montreal Voyageurs, combining hockey with full-time studies at the McGill University law school in Montreal. After being promoted to the NHL team he played in only six games before the Canadiens gave him the starting assignment in the 1971 Stanley Cup playoffs. After helping win the Cup, Ken worked with Nader's Raiders, the group of students who conducted research projects for consumer crusader Ralph Nader.

In 1971–72, Dryden continued to lead his double life. He returned to his law studies *and* the Montreal net, winning the Calder Trophy as the best rookie in the NHL and moving one step closer to his law degree. In the following year he played a starring role in the historic confrontation between Team Canada and the Soviet National Team, established himself as the NHL's number one goalie and completed his law studies at McGill.

Remarkably easy-going and relaxed in the midst of his whirlwind life, Dryden never viewed himself as anything special. "I've read stories that make me look like some sort of freak or

**Montreal rookie Ken Dryden makes a dramatic glove-tip save.**

superman," he said. "I think I'm a comparatively ordinary guy, who just happens to be participating in two fields of endeavor which I really like.

"People have said that I'm just playing hockey to pay my way through law school and when I have my degree, I'll quit hockey. Nothing could be farther from the truth. Hockey is a big challenge to me, and I love the game.

"Hockey always has had this great fable that players had to concentrate on the game, and another pursuit during the season would take away your concentration on the game. I think it's the exact opposite. I couldn't live with hockey twenty-four hours a day, 365 days a year. I doubt if I could live with law all the time, either."

Dryden was an outspoken critic of the Canadian system for developing professional hockey prospects. In the United States most pro football and basketball players get their athletic training and their education in one place—the university. But in Canada, where hockey is the number one sport, little has been done to encourage young athletes to continue their studies. The best athletic training grounds are found in the Junior A leagues, where hockey is played under minor pro conditions. As a result, few NHL hopefuls complete high school and fewer attend college.

"It's a very bad system," Dryden said. "A large majority of the kids who quit high school to concentrate on hockey never make it to the NHL. But they are stuck with a tenth grade education.

"It doesn't have to be that way. Hockey should be part of the education system in Canada with much more emphasis on the college level. It certainly wouldn't lower the quality of the game."

Ken and his older brother Dave (who also played in the NHL) were goalies from the time they started playing "road hockey" with the neighborhood boys in the Toronto suburb of Islington. In the driveway of the Dryden home the boys' father constructed nets from boards and chicken wire and provided tennis balls for "pucks."

Ken first started playing organized hockey in a league with older boys because his father felt he would improve more quickly against the stronger players. By the time he was 15, Ken was the leading goaltender in the Metro Toronto Junior B League, and the Montreal Canadiens, who had scouted him and placed his name on their negotiation list, wanted him on their Junior A team in Peterborough, Ontario.

"I was entering grade 13, the most important Ontario high school year," Dryden said. "Although I was tempted to move to Peterborough, I decided to stay at home, finish high school and play another season of Junior B hockey, plus high school basketball."

Dryden's high level of athletic and intellectual achievement attracted scholarship offers from several colleges. He chose Cornell, even though the school offered only an "honorary scholarship" of $200 a year instead of a full athletic scholarship. To finance the rest of his college costs Dryden worked as a waiter and dishwasher during the school year and on a construction crew in the summer.

Ken became a legend in U.S. college hockey during his three varsity seasons at Cornell, earning All-America honors each year. During that time the team lost only four of 83 games, and the lanky young netminder's goals-against average was an incredible 1.60. As a junior in 1967–68, Dryden yielded only 41 goals in 29 games.

In 1969 he graduated as a history major and joined the Canadian National Team based in Winnipeg. There he attended law school at the University of Manitoba. Ken had also been accepted at the Harvard Law School, and the Montreal Canadiens had offered him a professional contract. But he chose the national team because it gave him the chance to combine both hockey and education.

The Canadian National Team, which represented Canada in world amateur competition, was disbanded in the middle of the 1969–70 season after world hockey officials ruled that reinstated professionals would not be eligible to play in the world amateur tournament. Dryden finished his school year at Manitoba, then accepted a contract from the Canadiens which permitted him to attend Montreal's McGill University and play hockey with the Montreal Voyageurs, the Canadiens' team in the American Hockey League.

"The Canadiens realized then that I was serious about school," he said, "and my arrangement with them was that I'd attend McGill full time and play weekend games with the Voyageurs. I practiced with the team twice each week and made very few road trips. At Christmas, because I realized I could handle a heavier hockey load, I made the road trips and attended most workouts."

Mediocre goaltending had prevented the

Canadiens from climbing above third place in the NHL's East Division, so late in the season Dryden was promoted to the big league team. He played in six games before the season ended, all wins, and permitted only nine goals.

In the opening round of the 1971 playoffs the underdog Canadiens faced the mighty Boston Bruins, the defending Stanley Cup champions who had romped to first place during the regular schedule. Dryden was a surprise starter in the Montreal net during the first game at Boston, and even though the Canadiens lost that one, 3–1, Dryden showed he was ready for big league play.

In the second match Ken gave up five early goals. But then he brilliantly shut out the Bruins for the rest of the game. Meanwhile, the Canadiens scored six consecutive goals to earn a 7–5 victory.

The series see-sawed back and forth as Dryden repeatedly stopped the Bruins' great scorers, Phil Esposito and Bobby Orr. In the seventh and final game at Boston, Ken defended a 48-shot onslaught as Montreal won, 4–2, and eliminated the Bruins in one of the biggest upsets of modern hockey history.

"Dryden's catching hand was unbelievable," said the Bruins' Johnny McKenzie. "At least two dozen times in that series, we caught him out of position and shot for three-quarters of the empty net. Zap! That big mitt came out of thin air.

Twice, I had my stick in the air and was breaking into my goal-scoring dance when he did that."

Ken continued to excel as the Canadiens eliminated the Minnesota North Stars and played a tight, seven-game series against the Chicago Black Hawks to win the Stanley Cup. Dryden's dazzling performances earned him the Conn Smythe Trophy as the most valuable player in the playoffs.

**Dryden kicks away a shot by Chicago's Bobby Hull (9), and the Canadiens are on their way to another playoff victory in 1971.**

Dryden's main strengths as a goalie were his size and catching hand. At 6-foot-4 and 215 pounds, he filled a large portion of the net, and his ability to play the angles left very few openings for incoming attackers. Dryden had an 84-inch reach, which allowed him to catch shots that smaller goalies would have missed.

"When you come in on Dryden and he makes himself as large as possible between you and the goal, you're lucky to see the end of the rink, let alone a net opening to shoot at," commented Chicago's star center Stan Mikita. Despite his early success, Dryden felt he still had plenty to prove as a major league goalie. "To prove yourself in the NHL," he said, "you have to play several seasons, take the ups and downs, the knocks and bruises and survive the low points. I've had thoughts that I might be just a flash-in-the-pan because I only played well in six games and the playoffs."

Dryden spent the summer of '71 with "Nader's Raiders," organizing a clean water campaign with fishermen and allied businesses. Then before the 1971–72 season opened, he took his second-year law exams at McGill, which he had postponed in the spring when he was called to the Canadiens for the playoffs.

When the shooting started again, Dryden quickly proved he was no temporary star. He played in 64 of Montreal's 78 games (a staggering workload in a season when most teams divided the goal-tending chores evenly between two goalies). Dryden lost only eight of his starts and had a goals-against average of 2.24.

"I carried a full load of five courses at school and if I missed some lectures when I was on the road, I had a friend who loaned me his notes," Dryden said. "At times, the load was a little heavy. The team didn't gain much ground out of third place during the season, which made it frustrating."

In 1972 the Canadiens were unable to repeat their Stanley Cup heroics, losing a quarter-final series to the New York Rangers in six games. A Montreal newspaper ran a picture of Dryden after the concluding game, tears running down his face.

"You think the season is too long, and suddenly it's over," the disappointed goalie said. "Then you think it isn't long enough."

Dryden was an automatic selection for Team Canada to face the Soviet Union in the September 1972 series. The National Team of the Soviet Union had dominated world amateur hockey for a decade. Now Team Canada, a collection of the top National Hockey League stars, were challenging the Russians for world hockey supremacy. The winner would be determined after eight games—the first four to be played in Canada, the last four in Moscow.

Dryden had faced the Soviets in exhibition games during his stint with the Canadian National Team, and his record as a "big-game" NHL goalie made him an ideal choice for the short but crucial series. Most hockey people, including many players, expected the NHL stars to trounce the Soviets, but Dryden was one man who sounded a note of caution before the series opened.

"I hear people say that the Russians pass too much and don't shoot enough, that they can't do this and they can't do that in comparison to NHL players," he said. "Well, who says that they can't do everything? Maybe by NHL standards the Russians don't do things correctly, but they certainly do them properly by their standards. They'll be in superb condition and they are excellent players, just good athletes."

Team Canada quickly discovered that Dryden's estimation of the Soviet strength was correct. He had a shaky night in goal as the Russians opened the series with an impressive 7–3 victory, much to the amazement of the North American hockey world.

"We all had some ideas about the Soviets," said Dryden after that game. "But we were all surprised, and that surprise came early when we found out we couldn't put the pressure on them."

After the first four games in Canada, the Russians flew back to Moscow with two wins and one tie. The dismayed Canadian pros were traveling light, with just one victory in hand.

The goaltending chores for Team Canada

were being shared by Dryden and Tony Esposito of the Chicago Black Hawks. Esposito had starred in Team Canada's victory and tie. Dryden was the goalie against whom the Soviets had scored two convincing triumphs.

Things didn't look any better for Team Canada on the other side of the ocean. When the series shifted to the Soviet Union, Esposito was in the net for the opening (fifth) game. The NHL goalie saw his team's 4–1 lead vanish in the third period, when the Soviets rallied to a 5–4 victory. Five of the eight games were over, and the Canadians still had only one win.

But then things took a turn for the better. Dryden played magnificently in game six, which the Canadians won 3–2, and Esposito came on strong in the seventh game, which Team Canada won, 4–3, to even the series.

Immediately after the seventh game, Team Canada manager-coach Harry Sinden named Dryden as the starting goalie for the all-important final game. "Both goalies have played well under incredible pressure here," Sinden said. "But Dryden's record shows that he's been great in big games all his career."

The September 28, 1972, contest in Moscow's Palace of Sport was billed as "the most important hockey game in history." Each team had three victories, and the champions of hockey's first "world series" would be decided in a sudden-death match.

**Dryden gets his stick on the puck in the opening game of the 1972 series be-
tween Team Canada and the Soviet National Team.**

A succession of brilliant saves by Dryden in
the first two periods kept Team Canada in the
game, even though the Soviets led 5–3 entering
the final period. Dryden permitted no goals in
that period as his teammates came alive to tie
the game with two more goals. Then with just 34
seconds of play remaining, Paul Henderson of
the Toronto Maple Leafs blasted in the winning
goal. Team Canada had captured the series by
the narrowest of margins—but it was wide
enough for the new champions!

The key to Dryden's success in the Moscow

games was his ability to stop a favorite Soviet scoring maneuver. The Russian team often stationed an attacker at the side of Team Canada's net to deflect in quick passes, a move that produced several Soviet goals during the series. In the final game, Dryden managed to stop the play at least eight times.

"A goalie must weaken himself for other situations to handle that move," Dryden explained. "You have to play farther back in the net than usual to be in a position to stop the deflection."

Thus, with his extraordinary performance against the Soviet Nationals, another chapter was added to the unusual story of Ken Dryden, goaltender, scholar and crusader.

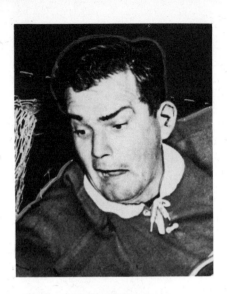

# BILL DURNAN
## Seven-Year Wonder

At the age of 27, big Bill Durnan emerged from the gold mines of Kirkland Lake in northern Ontario to become the golden boy of the Montreal Canadiens. Before that time he had played some junior league hockey and pitched the mining company's softball team to the Ontario championships. In later years he coached a senior hockey team in Ottawa and a junior team in Noranda, Quebec, before becoming a sales representative for a Canadian brewery. And sandwiched in between, Bill Durnan spent seven short years as the number one goalie in professional hockey.

No netminder in NHL history could match the list of accomplishments that Durnan racked up during those seven years, as he led the Canadiens to two Stanley Cups and four first-place finishes. In his rookie year Durnan won the Vezina Trophy and was named to the first All-Star team. The amazing goalie repeated both those feats five more times in the next six seasons. But then, at the peak of his career, Durnan left the limelight to run a resort hotel in Ottawa.

Ability, awards, honors—Bill Durnan appeared to have everything a professional athlete could want, yet the demands of his lonely job finally proved too much for him to overcome.

"Other players—defensemen and forwards

**Montreal's Bill Durnan makes a save against the Boston Bruins in 1947.**

—can make a mistake and someone covers up for them," Durnan once said. "If a goalie makes even the slightest error, the puck is in the net, and everyone knows it."

Bill Durnan was born in Toronto in 1916. He was a winning goalie from the time he played on boys' teams in Toronto. At the age of 14 he was starring for the North Toronto juniors, when the Toronto Maple Leafs offered him a spot on one of their junior teams. Durnan turned them down and got a job in Sudbury, Ontario, where he played junior hockey. His goaltending led the Sudbury Wolves to the Memorial Cup, awarded to the Canadian junior champions.

The Leafs kept Durnan on their reserve list and offered him a pro contract when he graduated from junior hockey. But when he twisted his knee while wrestling with a friend, the Leafs withdrew their offer. The disappointed Durnan decided to give up hockey.

Hockey wasn't Durnan's only talent. The young athlete was also one of Canada's best softball pitchers. In 1936 he moved to Kirkland Lake, a gold mining town in northern Ontario, where he apprenticed as a millwright and pitched for the company's softball team. Durnan's fine pitching helped lead Kirkland to several Ontario championships.

When the mining company signed several top senior amateur hockey players and formed the Kirkland Lake Blue Devils, Durnan was coaxed out of his "retirement" from hockey. The Blue Devils soon became a powerhouse team and won the Canadian championship in 1940.

The next year Durnan moved to Montreal, where he worked in the office of a steel company and played goal for the Montreal Royals, a senior amateur farm team of the NHL Canadiens. Although Durnan was obviously an NHL-caliber goalie, the Canadiens already had a top netminder in Paul Bibeault. Besides, Durnan had no plans for a career in pro hockey. But then North America got involved in World War II, and Bibeault joined the Canadian Army in 1943. Suddenly Montreal had a hole in their net. The Canadiens offered Durnan a contract.

Durnan was reluctant to accept it because he was earning a good combined salary from the Royals and the steel company, and he felt his future would be more secure there than in pro hockey. Canadien manager Tommy Gorman tried repeatedly to get Durnan's signature on an NHL contract, but the big goalie insisted that the salary wasn't large enough.

By the opening day of the 1943–44 NHL season, Durnan still hadn't signed. Ten minutes before game time Gorman finally agreed to meet Durnan's financial demands. Bill signed the contract and rushed into his uniform. Without a warm-up, he held the Boston Bruins to a 2–2 tie in his NHL debut.

His rookie season in the NHL was a tremendous success for Durnan—and for Montreal. In their 50-game schedule, the Canadiens won 38 and tied 7. Bill won the Vezina Trophy with a 2.18 goals-against average during the regular season and gave up only 14 goals in nine games as the Canadiens won the Stanley Cup playoffs.

Despite his excellent statistics, not everyone was impressed with Durnan's overnight success. Hockey fans and experts argued that his low goals-against average was misleading. They claimed that Durnan had not really been tested as an NHL goalie because he had never even faced the league's best players, who were thousands of miles away fighting in Europe and the Pacific. What would happen to Durnan, the critics wondered, when the super-scorers returned from the war?

It didn't take long for Durnan to answer that question. He repeated his Vezina Trophy triumph in 1944–45 and '45–46, even as the troops came home. When the war finally ended in September 1945, Bibeault returned to find his job gone, lost to the NHL's number one goalie—Bill Durnan. Bibeault was traded to Boston, and Durnan continued his winning ways in the Montreal net, where he picked up his fourth straight Vezina Trophy.

In an era when standing up straight and falling to the ice only in extreme emergencies was thought to be the best style for goalies, Durnan was a master of that approach. His bulky physique (6-feet, 195 pounds) allowed him to cover a large portion of the net, and he moved with surprising quickness for a man his size.

Durnan had another surprise for the opposing attackers—he was completely ambidextrous. He could hold the stick or catch the puck equally well with either hand. Goalies generally wear a glove with a wide, flat back on their stick hands and a baseball style "trapper" mitt on their catching hands. Both of Durnan's gloves were the same.

Steve Falconer, who coached Durnan in Toronto boys' hockey, had taught him to use both hands for all jobs. "Steve taught me that being ambidextrous was a big edge for a goalie," Bill explained. "Because I could hold the stick in both hands, I was always in the best position, no matter if the opponent coming in for a chance at my net was a left- or right-hand shot.

"Falconer would stand behind the net when our team was practicing and tap me on the shoulder when players came in for a shot. I'd shift the stick to that side."

Durnan finally met his match in 1946, the first time he faced an NHL rookie named Gordie Howe. When Howe approached the Canadiens' net, he had his stick in his normal right-hand position. But when Durnan shifted his goal-stick to that side, Howe quickly changed to a front-hand shot from the left side and scored. Howe, too,

**Durnan, an ambidextrous goalie, wears two baseball style "trapper" mitts.**

was ambidextrous and could deliver front-hand shots from either side. Before retiring in 1971, he set nearly all the NHL's career scoring records.

During the 1940s, the Canadiens and the Toronto Maple Leafs were the two strongest teams in the NHL, and their rivalry was a bitter one. The teams produced some of the finest hockey ever played, with classic confrontations between the firewagon Montrealers' high-speed attack and the tight-checking defense of the Maple Leafs. Between 1944 and 1949, Toronto won the Stanley Cup four times; the Canadiens claimed it twice.

An interesting contrast in style and personality was provided by the teams' superb goalies—Montreal's Bill Durnan and Toronto's Walter "Turk" Broda. Durnan was the classic stand-up goalie, an intense man with jittery nerves from the tension of the job. That pressure never bothered the chubby, happy-go-lucky Broda, who once fell asleep in the dressing room while the coach was delivering an emotional pregame pep talk.

Broda had little style and flopped to the ice a great deal. But although Durnan was more consistent and had a better average than Broda during most seasons, the Turk was a better clutch player. He earned a reputation as the greatest playoff netminder in history and had an edge on Durnan in Stanley Cup play.

"Probably our approach to the game—and our nervous systems—was the reason Turk Broda had a better playoff record than I did," Durnan said. "The pressure of the playoffs and worrying about soft goals used to make me jittery, but it never bothered the Turk. In fact, I can't remember anything ever bothering him. We were good friends off the ice, and I don't think Broda ever worried in his life. I wish I could have been that way."

One aspect of hockey that never worried Durnan much was practicing. The Montreal management often said that if Durnan had to be judged on his workout performances, he never would have made the NHL.

"Watching Bill in a practice was almost a joke," said Toe Blake, the Canadiens' star center who later became the team's coach. "He didn't even try to stop shots, although occasionally when he felt he wasn't playing too well, he'd bear down a little. But when a game started, he'd stop shots with his head if he had to."

When the Canadiens finished the 1947–48 season in fifth place and missed the playoffs, Durnan began to think of retiring. The critical Montreal fans had booed Durnan several times during the year as if he alone were to blame for the team's sag. Fortunately, the Canadien management was able to convince their netminder to ignore the fans, and Durnan went on to his greatest season ever. In 1948–49, he won still another Vezina Trophy and first All-Star team selection. To top it all off, late that season Durnan established a modern goaltending record which may never be broken. During 309 minutes and 21 seconds of play he didn't yield a single goal. His incredible streak included four consecutive shutouts.

Durnan had another fine season in 1949–50. His goals-against average was an excellent 2.20, and he won his sixth Vezina Trophy and All-Star selection. But even though he played with his usual cool approach, the high-strung goalie's nerves were on edge all the time.

Late in the season Durnan dropped to the ice

to smother a loose puck in a game at Chicago and suffered a severe cut to his head from a skate blade. He was also having trouble with a painful hand injury.

When the New York Rangers won the first three games of the semi-final playoff series from Montreal, Durnan asked the Canadiens' coach Dick Irvin to replace him in goal. He said his nerves were very bad and he had dizzy spells from the skate cut on his head.

Back-up goalie Gerry McNeil took over the net, and the Canadiens won the fourth game. However, the Rangers won the next game, and the series.

Big Bill Durnan had seemed bullet-proof, immune to the pressures of playing goal in the National Hockey League. But not even the great Durnan had strong enough nerves to withstand the stresses of his position. On the train going back to Montreal, Durnan told the Canadiens' managing-director Frank Selke that he was finished with hockey for good.

"I'm nervous and jittery, and I don't want to crack up all at once," Durnan said. "I want to enjoy my family life while I have my health. I could wait until they kick me out, but I don't want to jeopardize the team's chances."

"Bill always felt a big responsibility toward the team," said a teammate. "Giving up goals always bothered him, especially if he figured he had a chance of stopping a shot that beat him.

**After faking Durnan out of position, Don Raleigh of the New York Rangers slams the puck into the Montreal net.**

When he thought he wasn't playing as well as he could, he quit hockey because he didn't want to hurt the other players' chances of winning."

"It was time for me to get out, that's all," Durnan said. "I couldn't sleep before games, and I couldn't sleep after them. I was tense all the time."

For several years after his retirement Durnan owned and operated a hotel in Ottawa and coached the senior Ottawa Senators. He also coached a junior team in Noranda, Quebec, and had a successful five years as coach of the Kitchener, Ontario, Dutchmen. He later worked as a sales representative for a brewery.

Durnan was elected to the Hockey Hall of

Fame in 1964. A few years later his health began to fail. The deaths of those two great rivals of the 1940s, Durnan and Turk Broda, came within a month of each other in the autumn of 1972. It was the end of an era in pro hockey. But a whole new generation of NHL goalies would spend years trying to match the amazing achievements of Bill Durnan.

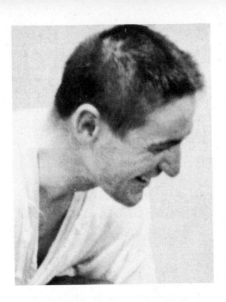

# TERRY SAWCHUK
## Medical Miracle

It would take two long lists to record all the milestones in the incredible NHL career of Terry Sawchuk. One list would cover his achievements, and the other would include his injuries.

Sawchuk played in 971 games during his long professional career. In 20 years he played for five NHL teams (the Detroit Red Wings, Boston Bruins, Toronto Maple Leafs, Los Angeles Kings and New York Rangers) and compiled an overall goals-against average of 2.52. His 103 career shutouts set an NHL record that seemed likely to stand for many years. He won the Vezina Trophy as top goalie four times and earned

**Terry Sawchuk lies unconscious near the Red Wing net after being hit by a puck in a 1960 game against the Montreal Canadiens.**

seven All-Star team nominations, three of them to the first team.

The assortment of injuries which Sawchuk suffered throughout his lifetime included just about everything in a medical textbook. "Medical science should take Sawchuk," a teammate once

94

said, "because research could be conducted on him in 27 ailments at one time."

Sawchuk's medical problems began long before he entered the league. At the age of twelve, Terry broke his right arm. The break didn't heal properly, and the arm remained several inches shorter than the left arm. When he was a rookie in minor professional hockey his right eye was severely damaged and only emergency surgery saved his sight. An arthritic shoulder and neuritis in his legs caused frequent problems throughout his career.

Terry seemed no safer off the ice than on it. In a 1954 auto accident several of his ribs were broken and one of his lungs collapsed. Then in 1967 Sawchuk came down with mononucleosis, the weakening viral infection that is often brought on by overwork or extreme stress. And for many years herniated discs in his back caused Sawchuk to walk with a stooped-over stance.

His injury list also included many that are associated with goaltending—several broken fingers, cuts to hand tendons, a broken shoulder, muscle sprains and pulls, and countless facial cuts which required more than 400 stitches. The strain of the job also caused him to lose weight and lose sleep. It was often a wonder that he was able to play at all.

When he first joined the Red Wings in 1950, Sawchuk was a chubby 200-pounder with a carefree, breezy approach to life. Ten years later he was a scrawny 160 pounds and had turned into a moody, brooding man, who frequently was short tempered with hockey writers and fans.

Sawchuk was born in 1929 in Winnipeg, Manitoba, where he started playing goal in pee wee hockey. The Detroit Red Wings sponsored the minor hockey system in East Kildonan, the Winnipeg suburb where Sawchuk grew up, and the Wing scouts were very impressed with the young goalie's potential.

Sawchuk played one season of Junior A hockey with Detroit's farm team at Windsor. Then at age 17 he turned professional with the Omaha Knights of the old U.S. Hockey League.

"Terry was very young to be a professional goalie," Detroit manager Jack Adams said. "But he was so good that he would have been wasting his time if he remained in junior hockey."

Sawchuk quickly proved that Adams' judgment was correct. The young goalie was named Rookie-of-the-Year in 1947–48 when he compiled a 3.22 average at Omaha. The Wings promoted him to their American League farm club at Indianapolis, and again he was voted best rookie in that league. Sawchuk spent two successful seasons at Indianapolis before he was called up to Detroit to replace the Wings' injured Harry Lumley during the 1949–50 season. The young sub looked as good in the NHL as he had in the minors, allowing only 16 goals in seven games.

The Red Wings created a starting spot for

Sawchuk in the 1950–51 season when they traded the veteran Lumley to Toronto. At 20 years of age Sawchuk became the goaltender on a power-house Detroit team that was the dominant NHL club of the early 1950s. He had a tremendous rookie year in the big league, allowing a meager 1.98 goals per game and recording eleven shut-outs. He missed winning the Vezina Trophy by one goal but was a unanimous selection for the Calder award as best rookie.

Sawchuk brought a new style of goaltending to the NHL. Until he arrived, goalies were ex-pected to stand erect, bending slightly at the knees. Sawchuck stood with his waist bent al-most at a right angle, a style that Detroit's man-ager Adams tried to change. But Sawchuk was

**In a typical pose, rookie Sawchuk guards the Detroit net.**

convinced that his approach was the best for the modern game of hockey, and his successful performances eventually put a stop to Adams' criticism.

"I was able to move much more quickly from the crouch position," Sawchuk explained. "I had better balance to move both legs, especially when I had to kick out my leg to stop a shot. When I broke into the NHL, the style of hockey was changing with many more scrambles in front of the net and shots from the point. This led to a greatly increased number of screen shots, which I couldn't see while standing straight up. From the crouch I was able to see the puck much sooner if it came through a scramble of players."

During his first five NHL seasons, Sawchuk's goals-against average was below 2.00 each year and he had 54 shutouts. One of his most remarkable feats came when the Wings won the 1952 Stanley Cup, winning eight straight games over Toronto and Montreal. Sawchuk allowed only five goals and had four shutouts.

Things went well for Sawchuk in those years as he managed to avoid any serious injuries. But when he appeared at the Wings' training camp one autumn with 230 pounds on his 5-foot-11 frame, manager Adams put him on a strict diet. Sawchuk lost 40 pounds, weight he never was able to regain. His friends claimed that Sawchuk's personality changed with the big weight loss. His cheery outlook on life disappeared, and he became an unhappy loner.

By 1955 injuries and bad nerves made Sawchuk's future a question mark, and Detroit traded him to Boston in a deal that shocked the hockey world. Although Detroit had a splendid young goalie, Glenn Hall, to replace him, many rivals questioned the wisdom of dealing away the NHL's top goaltender.

Sawchuk's two seasons with the Bruins were not happy ones. He was very lonely in Boston because his wife and children had remained at their home in Detroit. Nevertheless, Terry played superbly with the fifth-place Bruins and had a 2.66 average plus nine shutouts.

From the start of the 1956–57 season Sawchuk seemed thin and jittery, although he was still playing well. He frequently quarrelled with the critical Boston sportswriters and even threatened a lawsuit over stories written about him.

Early in January 1957, Sawchuk told the Bruins' manager Milt Schmidt that he was fed up with hockey. A week later he announced his retirement from the game at a press conference. "My nerves are shot," Sawchuk said. "I can't eat, I can't sleep and I'm edgy all the time. There were many times this season when I didn't think I could finish a game, so I'm getting out."

Doctors soon discovered that Sawchuk was completely exhausted and on the verge of a nervous breakdown. Later, tests revealed that he had mononucleosis. He didn't play for the remainder of the season, but his "retirement" didn't last long. A chain of circumstances saw Sawchuk return to the Red Wings. Glenn Hall had played superbly in the Detroit net for two seasons, but when he had a poor playoff series, the team management reasoned that he wasn't a good clutch goalie and decided to trade him. Looking for a replacement, Detroit manager Adams turned to the man he had dealt away in 1955.

Sawchuk was enthused about returning to hockey if he could rejoin the Red Wings. The Detroit team traded Hall to Chicago and winger Johnny Bucyk to Boston in exchange for Sawchuk.

"I never enjoyed Boston," Sawchuk said. "I was away from my wife and family. We didn't want to move the kids because they were doing well in school in Detroit. I don't think I would have played hockey again if I hadn't been traded back to the Wings."

Sawchuk was happy to be back in Detroit, and he performed well for the Red Wings over the next seven seasons, despite a discouraging series of injuries.

After Jacques Plante of the Montreal Canadiens pioneered the face mask for goalies in 1959, the accident-prone Sawchuk was the first goalie to use one. "I found that I had much more confidence with the mask," Sawchuk said. "I could dive into pile-ups in front of the net and not worry about being cut in the face by a stick or a skate. There were always a few guys in the NHL who would shoot at a goalie's head, trying to scare him. They didn't worry me after I started to wear the mask."

Another thing that made life easier for Sawchuk was the introduction of the two-goalie system in the mid-1960s. That was especially important to Sawchuk because he needed the rest between starting assignments to recuperate from his constant injuries. Sawchuk shared the net with Hank Bassen for several seasons. Then Detroit acquired Roger Crozier, an excellent young goalie. Sawchuk's back ailment forced him out of the line-up in 1963–64, and Crozier got a chance to show his ability.

When the Red Wings decided to protect Bassen and Crozier in the 1964 draft, the Maple Leafs claimed Sawchuk. Although Terry was 35 at the time, the Leafs paid $30,000 for his services. Sawchuk proved the Leafs had made a good deal when he and Johnny Bower (who was 41 at the time) combined to win the Vezina Trophy in the 1964–65 season. The two old-timers continued to supply excellent goaling between injuries for the Leafs over the next two seasons.

In 1965–66, Sawchuk endured two complicated operations to correct problems in his back and spine. The first surgery in the summer of 1966 straightened his back and made it possible for him to stand erect for the first time in several years. That operation added two inches to his height.

Early in the season Terry's back pains returned and a second operation in December 1966 was required to repair the damage. Sawchuk had to follow a long physiotherapy program before he could play again. There were many times during the year when Terry figured his playing days were over, but he battled back to rejoin the Leafs late in the schedule and became the first NHL goalie to record 100 career shutouts.

Bower had also battled injuries all year, and the Maple Leafs finished an unimpressive third in the standings. They had qualified for the Stanley Cup playoffs, but no one expected them to be serious contenders for the trophy.

The opening playoff round sent the Leafs against the first-place Black Hawks. After the teams split the first four games, Bower drew the goaling assignment for the Leafs in the critical fifth game at Chicago. The Hawks took a 2–1 lead early in the game. Then Bower was injured, and Terry Sawchuk took over in goal.

Just minutes after Sawchuk came in, a slap shot from the stick of Chicago's mighty Bobby Hull struck Terry on the shoulder. For several minutes he could barely move his arm. "At first I figured somebody had stabbed me with a red-hot poker," Sawchuk recalled.

Despite his injury Sawchuk finished the

game with what many experts called the finest exhibition of goaltending in the game's history. The Black Hawk offense fired 37 shots at Sawchuk, but the veteran goalie made one dazzling save after another. Three times Sawchuk deprived Bobby Hull of sure goals by diving across the net to stop his shots, and through the last two periods he held the powerful Hawks scoreless. The Leafs scored three times and won 4–2.

"It was the only time in my career when I ever scored three goals and the red light didn't go on," said Hull after the game.

In the sixth match Sawchuk played another superb game as the Leafs eliminated Chicago with a 3–1 victory. The third-place Leafs had reached the finals—but to win the Cup they would have to beat heavily favored Montreal.

Led by Sawchuk in four games and Bower in two, the determined Toronto team surprised the experts and delighted their fans with an upset triumph over mighty Montreal. Although the Canadiens held a decided edge in two games, they were unable to get past Sawchuk when it counted most.

"Winning that Stanley Cup was the biggest thrill of my life," Sawchuk said. "I had almost a complete physical breakdown during the season, and the recovery period was long and discouraging. I'll admit there were times—many of them,

Between injuries, Sawchuk has some good moments with the Los Angeles Kings. Here he knocks away a shot by Pittsburgh's Ken Schinkel (12).

in fact—when I figured I'd never play hockey again. Sometimes I wondered if I'd be able to walk properly."

Following his Stanley Cup heroics, Sawchuk considered retirement. However, in the 1967 expansion draft the Los Angeles Kings claimed

104

him. The new team needed an experienced goalie and was willing to pay whatever was necessary to get one. When the Kings offered Sawchuk a $40,000 contract, the best salary of his career, the veteran netminder moved to California where he helped the team to a strong second-place finish in the new division.

Terry was playing well—whenever he was healthy enough to play. But when a new crop of injuries kept him out of the line-up several times, the Kings decided they needed a younger man. They traded him back to Detroit for his third stint with the Red Wings.

Sawchuk didn't stay in Detroit for long. In fact, he played in only ten games as substitute for Roger Crozier. At the end of the 1968–69 season he was traded again—this time to the New York Rangers, where he played behind Ed Giacomin. Sawchuk played just eight games during his last NHL season, but he managed to record his 103rd shutout.

Accidents and injuries had plagued Sawchuk throughout his career. The final injury occured during the offseason. Sawchuk suffered internal injuries from a bad fall one day in May 1970 and died soon after from a blood clot in an artery.

"I saw a lot of great goalies in the NHL," said the Rangers' manager-coach Emile Francis, himself a former big league goalie. "But I think Terry Sawchuk probably was the best goalie who ever played the game."

In June 1971, Terry Sawchuk was voted into the Hockey Hall of Fame, a fitting tribute to the goalie who overcame an incredible string of hardships to become a master of his craft.

# GERRY CHEEVERS
## In a League by Himself

The Cleveland Crusaders were an unusual collection of players when they made their 1972 debut in the opening game of the World Hockey Association schedule. Cleveland was a late entry in the WHA, the twelve-team league that hoped to rival the established National Hockey League. For the most part Cleveland's roster was made up of men on their way up—or on their way down. Some were former minor league stars, eager for an opportunity to play major league hockey; others had been lured away from the NHL by large contract offers.

**New York Raiders and Cleveland Crusaders tangle at the net as Gerry Cheevers (lower right) stops a Raider goal attempt.**

The goaltending position, however, was one spot the Crusaders had covered in top style. Gerry Cheevers, who had helped the mighty Boston Bruins to Stanley Cup victories in two of the three previous seasons, stood before the net as the players were introduced to the wildly cheering Cleveland fans. The veteran goalie was as nervous as a rookie.

"First, it was a very big decision for me to leave the Bruins, who had given me the chance to play and succeed in the NHL, and jump to the new league," Cheevers later explained. "Then, the fact that it was the first game in a rather historic happening, the opening of a new hockey league, made it rather special. I wanted to start big and show the fans in Cleveland something."

Cheevers couldn't have hoped for a bigger show than the one he put on. He picked up a shutout as the Crusaders scored a 2–0 win over the Quebec Nordiques. Gerry Cheevers, the Cleveland Crusaders and the new World Hockey Association were all off to a fine start. But the goalie, the team and the league might never even have gotten together if it hadn't been for one man: a dynamic sports promoter named Nick Mileti.

When the new league was first conceived, Mileti already owned most of Cleveland's sports teams—the baseball Indians, the basketball Cavaliers and American Hockey League's Barons. But for years the Cleveland entrepreneur had dreamed of acquiring a major league hockey team. He first applied to the NHL for one of the two new franchises to be added in the 1972 expansion program, but that bid was unsuccessful. The new franchises, scheduled to begin play in 1973–74, were awarded to Washington and Kansas City.

Mileti then turned to the brand new World Hockey Association, which was having some trouble finding a suitable location for its twelfth team. The franchise had originally been set for Calgary, Alberta, but at the last minute the backers in that city had withdrawn their support and the team had collapsed. So the WHA organizers were more than glad to do business with the lively and successful Mileti.

110

By the time the Cleveland operator got his franchise the other WHA teams already had a good head start in their recruiting programs. Mileti quickly caught up by signing an assortment of NHL and minor league players, but the man he really wanted for his team was Gerry Cheevers. The 31-year-old Cheevers was then in the prime of his goaltending career.

Cheevers, however, was happily playing with the powerhouse Boston Bruins along with such superstars as Bobby Orr and Phil Esposito. Although the Bruins' devastating offense usually overshadowed the achievements of the club's defensemen and goalies, Gerry's performance during the 1971–72 season had propelled him into the front ranks of NHL goalies.

That year Cheevers had established an NHL record by playing undefeated in 32 straight games to smash the previous mark of 23 set by another Bruin goalie, Frank Brimsek, in 1940–41. In his 41 Bruin games Cheevers helped Boston to 27 wins and eight ties.

The 1972–73 contract negotiations between Boston and Cheevers were well underway when Mileti and the Crusaders entered the picture. The Bruins were prepared to pay Gerry $70,000 plus bonuses, but their offer was dwarfed by Cleveland's offer. After a month of meetings Cheevers finally signed with the Crusaders for a total of $1,400,000—$200,000 per season for seven years.

"I'm sorry to be leaving the Bruins because we were a very closely knit team in Boston and the organization always treated me well," Cheevers said. "I had to weigh a great many things on both sides before reaching a decision. My priorities came down to one thing, and that was security for my family. Cleveland offered that in the form of a long-term, high-paying contract."

The Bruins were not about to surrender their star goalie without a fight. They asked the U.S. courts for an injunction that would forbid Cheevers and center Derek Sanderson (who had signed a $2,600,000 contract with the WHA's Philadelphia Blazers) to join their new teams.

In a Boston hearing, U. S. District Court Judge Andrew Caffery said he had to consider the financial rewards that the players might gain by jumping to the new league as well as the damage the Bruins might suffer without them. Then, after studying both sides of the conflict, Judge Caffery ruled in favor of the players. Cheevers and Sanderson were free to move to the new league. However, they would not be permitted to make any personal appearances on behalf of the WHA clubs or to practice with their new teams until October 1, 1972, the day their 1971–72 Bruin contracts expired.

As soon as his contract ran out, Cheevers joined the Crusaders' training camp. The 1972–73 season was only a week away. "I felt all along that we would win the case, but I had a few small doubts," Cheevers said. "I was worried that I wouldn't get back in the groove by the time the season started. It takes time for a goalie to get his timing and balance just right."

Gerry Cheevers had spent a good part of his lifetime perfecting his hockey skills. He was born in St. Catharines, Ontario, in 1940. His father, Joe Cheevers, was one of Canada's greatest lacrosse players and a member of the Canadian Sports Hall of Fame. As a young boy Gerry played all sports, but lacrosse and hockey were his favorites.

When he was 16, Cheevers went to St. Michael's College in Toronto, a boys' school which fielded a Junior A hockey team under the sponsorship of the Toronto Maple Leafs. Cheevers spent his first three years at St. Michael's with the school's Junior B team. In the 1959–60 season he became first-string goalie with the St. Michael's Majors in the Ontario Junior A league and won the leading goalie award with a fine 3.06 average against some tough competition.

The following season Cheevers was a star performer in the Majors' steady advance to the Canadian junior championship. In the middle of the schedule the team's coach, Father David Bauer, switched Cheevers to the wing for an eight-game stretch.

"Playing goal over a long season can get to

be a bit boring for a young player," Father Bauer explained. "Gerry was a strong skater and he liked to body-check. Besides, goalies need to know how to handle the puck in modern hockey."

Cheevers' accomplishments in junior hockey appeared to make him an excellent candidate for the Leaf net. But even though the Maple Leafs always had a productive farm system, almost all their NHL goalies had been picked up in trades with other teams. During his four years in the Toronto farm system, Cheevers played only two games for the NHL club.

The young goalie made a variety of minor league stops—Sault Ste. Marie, Pittsburgh, Sudbury and Rochester. He had two outstanding seasons in Rochester with the Leafs' top farm team in the American Hockey League and was the AHL's leading goalie in 1964–65. Despite Cheevers' success the Leafs decided to stick with their older goalies, Bower and Sawchuk. They even got a third experienced goalie, Bruce Gamble.

When Cheevers was unprotected in the 1965 intra-league draft, the Bruins claimed him. "I wasn't a bit surprised when the Leafs dropped me," Cheevers said. "They had Bower and Sawchuk, both established goalies, and when they added Gamble, I knew I was gone. Gamble was a proven, experienced pro goalie, and I was just a young prospect. Maybe I was going to develop, and maybe I wasn't."

Cheevers spent part of his first two seasons in the Boston organization with the Bruins and part with their Central League farm club at Oklahoma City. Like the Maple Leafs, the Bruins were deep in goalies. Veteran Eddie Johnston was the starting netminder, and there were two other top young prospects, Bernie Parent and Doug Favell.

Gerry's appearances with the Bruins were limited at first. But when the Bruins were allowed to protect just two of their goalies from the 1967 draft which would stock the NHL's six new expansion teams, they chose Johnston and Cheevers. "It was a great boost to my confidence," Gerry recalled, "because I realized then that the Bruins figured I had the stuff to be an NHL goalie. I thought I had the ability, but it was a question of showing what I could do."

Given the opportunity to perform on a good NHL team, Cheevers quickly proved he belonged in the major leagues by maintaining a 2.83 goals-against average in the 1967–68 season.

The rise of the Boston Bruins to a position of prominence in the NHL and Gerry Cheevers' climb to the front rank of goalies went hand in hand. After an eight-year slump in which the team had failed to reach the playoffs, the Bruins suddenly became a contending club. Bobby Orr arrived in Boston in 1967, and a big trade brought Phil Esposito, Ken Hodge and Fred

Stanfield to the Bruins from the Chicago Black Hawks.

Cheevers was about to take his place with one of the greatest hockey teams ever assembled. But because the team scored so many goals, the netminders were overshadowed by the scoring stars. Maintaining a low goals-against average on the attack-oriented club was a difficult task for the goalies, but both Cheevers and Johnston managed to achieve respectable figures.

**Playing with the Boston Bruins, Cheevers comes out of the net to deflect a shot by Dennis Hull of the Chicago Black Hawks.**

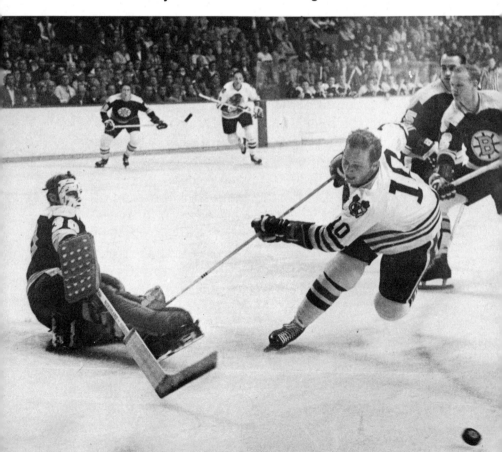

Cheevers' best performances came in the big matches, and he soon established a reputation as a "clutch" goalie. In the 1969 playoffs, for example, he allowed only 16 goals in nine games and had three shutouts.

In 1970 the Bruins won their first Stanley Cup in 29 years. Cheevers was in the net for all twelve playoff wins, including ten consecutive victories. Even that great performance was overshadowed by the work of the Boston scoring machine.

Then the Bruins were upset by the Montreal Canadiens in the 1971 quarter-finals. The loss was blamed on poor goaltending. The real cause of the Bruin defeat was Montreal goalie Ken Dryden. The Canadien netminder performed a string of miracles to stop the Bruin superscorers.

"The people who blamed our goaltending for the loss just didn't know what they were talking about," said the Bruins' coach Tom Johnson. "Sure, it was goaltending that beat us—Dryden's goaltending!"

Any questions about Boston's strength in goal were convincingly answered by Cheevers during the 1971–72 season. The Bruin goalie compiled an amazing record of 32 consecutive undefeated games.

"Gerry's record was incredible," said his goaling partner Johnston, "but nobody bothered too much about it. If he had been on any team other than the Bruins, where the players didn't

117

**In the 1972 playoffs Gerry catches the puck on the tip of his glove to rob Ranger Pete Stemkowski of a goal.**

score as many goals, he'd be earning raves."

"I laugh when anyone talks about our supposedly weak goaltending," said coach Johnson. "Any time we were in trouble, Cheevers and Johnston held us in the game until we got our attack going. Goals-against average is sometimes a very deceiving way to measure a goalie's value to his team. It's what he does in a particular game situation—the big saves he makes that keep his team in contention—that really counts."

118

Cheevers, who normally had a very easy-going approach to his high-pressure profession, bristled when mention was made of the team's supposedly mediocre goaltending. "During the last three years, we've finished first three times and won the Stanley Cup twice," he declared. "Bad goaltending didn't do that."

In the 1972 playoffs Cheevers and Johnston split the goaling chores and had a 2.26 average. When the Bruins clinched the Cup by shutting out the New York Rangers, 3–0, in the last game of their hectic final, there was no doubt that Cheevers was the game's brightest star.

Cheevers left Boston after completing his greatest season ever. Because of his excellent record as a clutch performer, Cheevers' loss was an especially big blow to the Bruins.

Gerry went on to become a key player for the Crusaders, both on the ice and as team leader in the dressing room. His flamboyant style of goaltending made him a big favorite with the Cleveland fans. Blessed with extraordinary reflexes, Gerry had one of the best catching hands among pro goalies. He was also an expert at journeying far from the net to trap loose pucks. Frequently he would go to the boards or almost to the blueline to beat an opponent to the puck. Cheevers' excellent skating and his experience as a forward in junior hockey added an extra dimension to his goaltending abilities.

"I'm not a conservative type of goalie who

always stays close to the crease," Cheevers said. "If I see the chance to skate out and gain possession of a loose puck in our zone, then I'll take that chance. I figure a goalie has to move out and challenge the shooters, too."

If Cheevers was looking for a challenge, he had come to the right place. The fledgling WHA would need all the help it could get in its uphill fight against the well-established NHL. And Gerry Cheevers had plenty of help to offer. Throughout the 1972–73 season he was the new league's number one goalie as he continued the dazzling play that had made him a winner in the NHL.

Cheevers' goals-against average in the offense-oriented league was a strong 2.85 per game, and his excellent play was the major reason for the Crusaders' second-place finish in the Eastern Division. Cheevers became a big favorite with the Cleveland fans, who turned out in large numbers to make the franchise one of the WHA's most successful.

# GUMP WORSLEY
## The Answer Man

Sometimes it was hard to take Lorne (Gump) Worsley seriously. Even though he was one of the NHL's greatest goalies, he was better known for his sharp wit than for his outstanding puck-blocking ability. Throughout his long career, the fun-loving goalie turned even the most serious situations into a joke. Sportswriters and radio and television commentators loved to interview the wisecracking goalie who had an answer for every question.

Worsley was once asked if there were any hockey rules he would like to see changed. "What they should do," Gump replied, "is pass a rule that bans shots on goal. Then a goalie would have it easier."

Worsley was once struck on the head by one of Bobby Hull's mighty slap-shots. The flat side of the puck hit Worsley and knocked him unconscious. When asked what would have happened if the edge of the puck had hit him, Worsley quipped, "Just call the undertaker and tell him to bring over a box for my body."

Even Worsley's appearance was funny. His chunky build made it hard to believe that he was really an excellent athlete. At 5-foot-7 and 185 pounds, he had a pot belly and heavy jowls. His crewcut hairstyle made his head look too big for his body and added to his image as a clown. Strangely enough, as a young boy Worsley had been so skinny that his pals nicknamed him "Gump" after the cartoon character Andy Gump.

During Gump's ten-year stint with the Rangers in the 1950's, he and New York coach Phil Watson carried on a long-running verbal battle. When a newspaper story revealed that Watson had called his pudgy goalie a "beer belly," Worsley vehemently denied the charge. "How can he call me a beer belly when I don't drink beer?" he said. "I only drink whiskey!"

Worsley's comical exterior and his light-hearted approach to life almost made people forget that he was a superior goalie. But on the ice, Worsley was all business. His cat-quickness, his fearlessness and his enormous competitive fire

**Gump the Answer Man has a few questions for the referee.**

made Gump Worsley one of the top NHL goal-tenders during his 20-year career with the New York Rangers, Montreal Canadiens and Minnesota North Stars.

"People who didn't know Gump would see him clowning around and hear him making jokes," said his long-time New York roommate Andy Bathgate. "They figured he wasn't serious about anything. But no better competitor—and few better goalies—ever played in this league."

Lorne Worsley was born in the Montreal suburb of Point St. Charles in 1929. Life was hard for the family because his father, an iron-worker, was unemployed for four years during the depression.

"We never had much money when I was a kid, but I had a lot of fun," Worsley recalled. "I was always playing a sport—soccer, football, baseball or hockey, and I shot a lot of pool. When I was playing with the Canadiens, I used to drop out to Point St. Charles every week and shoot the breeze with my old pals—the ones who weren't in jail."

Worsley began goaltending in playground hockey games. Later he moved up to the junior league Verdun Cyclones where the New York Ranger scouts spotted him and placed his name on their negotiation list.

The young goalie spent two seasons with the New York Rovers in the Eastern Amateur

League and was practice goalie for the Rangers. In 1950 he turned professional with the St. Paul Saints and was the leading goalie in the old U. S. Hockey League. Following that came an excellent season with the Saskatoon Quakers in the Western League.

Worsley won the first-string job with the Rangers in 1952–53, and that season he received the Calder Trophy as the NHL's top rookie. But the next year he lost the Ranger job to Johnny Bower and was demoted to the Vancouver Canucks of the Western League, where he compiled a record 2.40 average. Finally, in 1954–55, Gump came back to the Rangers to stay.

In Gump's ten seasons in New York the Rangers finished in the bottom half of the league and missed the playoffs six times. New York was a weak team that was usually out-muscled by its larger opponents. Worsley had to face a barrage of shots—often as many as 50—behind a porous defense and weak-checking forwards. In many games he stood almost alone as strong opponents swarmed his net. Despite the heavy workload, Worsley maintained a respectable goals-against average and, of course, his sense of humor.

When Worsley was asked which NHL team gave him the most trouble, he answered without any hesitation: "The Rangers!" Years later, he became part owner of a restaurant in his hometown of Montreal and put a "Ranger Special" on the menu. The dish was chicken salad.

"In many ways those were good years for me in New York," Gump said. "Because the team was going nowhere, and fast, too, there wasn't much pressure on a goalie. I just did the best I could and didn't worry about a thing."

On a June afternoon in 1963, Worsley was sitting in the backyard of his Montreal home when a neighbor rushed in to tell him that the Rangers had traded him to Montreal.

"The night before, I'd met the Rangers' general manager, Muzz Patrick, and we'd had a few laughs," Worlsey said. "I asked him as a joke if he planned to trade me. He said he couldn't because I was a fixture in New York. I told him that if he did trade me, I wanted to go to Montreal.

"It was just a gag and I forgot about it when I went home that night. But the next day my neighbor told me he'd heard on the radio that the Rangers had traded me, Dave Balon, Leon Rochefort and Len Ronson to the Canadiens for Jacques Plante, Phil Goyette and Don Marshall. I thought he was joking until I heard it on the radio myself."

Worsley wasn't the only one amazed by the news. The trade shocked the whole hockey world because Montreal's Jacques Plante had been the NHL's number one goalie, winner of the Vezina Trophy six times in the last eight seasons. But the Canadiens' coach Toe Blake had lost patience with Plante's claims of frequent injuries and considered the goalie an exasperating hypochondriac.

"I was very surprised by the whole thing," Worsley said. "I was 34 years old at the time and hadn't exactly been a big winner in New York. I was really looking forward to joining a top team."

Worsley's first season in Montreal wasn't a happy one. He had played only eight games with the Canadiens when he pulled a hamstring muscle and missed two weeks of action. While Worsley was sidelined Charlie Hodge, a veteran goalie who had played in Plante's shadow, won the starting job. The Gumper was sent to the Quebec Aces in the American Hockey League. He spent most of the 1963–64 campaign there while Hodge was winning the Vezina Trophy in Montreal.

Worsley opened the 1964–65 season with Quebec but was recalled by the Canadiens when Hodge needed a rest. Late in the season his promotion became permanent, and Worsley played an important role in the Canadiens' bid for the Stanley Cup.

Worsley was drinking a cup of coffee when coach Blake told him that he was to be the starting goalie for the decisive seventh game in the final against Chicago. "When he told me that, I was so nervous that my hands started to shake," Worsley quipped. "It was the first time I ever saw whitecaps in a coffee cup."

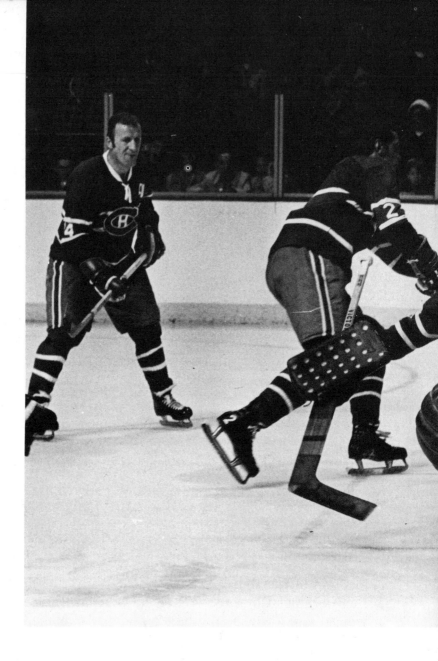

**Worsley deflects a Ranger shot—the puck is at far right.**

Despite his nervousness, Gump came through in the crucial game, and the Canadiens won the Cup. In his eight playoff games he allowed only 14 goals as Montreal eliminated the Toronto Maple Leafs and the Chicago Black Hawks.

Worsley's first big season with the Canadiens had been a great success. After ten years with the Rangers, the perennial NHL doormats, Gump really appreciated the help he was getting from the solid Canadien defensemen. "On the ice it was a different story than New York," Gump explained. "I'll tell you, it seemed easy to have maybe 25 shots in a game after some of those nights I spent in the Ranger net."

In 1965–66 Gump played in 51 games for the Canadiens and had a 2.36 goals-against average as he and Hodge combined to win the Vezina Trophy. Worsley was named as goalie on the second All-Star team, his first nomination. In the playoffs he led Montreal to another Stanley Cup, allowing just 20 goals in ten games.

But despite his fine achievements, Worsley was beginning to feel the tremendous pressures of playing goal. In New York, the Rangers had attracted little attention from anyone but their most devoted fans. In Montreal, however, things were much different. The Canadiens were the top sport team in the city, and a legion of supporters closely watched their every move.

"It was harder to play in Montreal than in

New York for one reason: in Montreal, you had to win," Worsley said. "People recognized hockey players everywhere they went in Montreal. If we lost two games in a row, you hated to walk down the street because many people would stop you to ask what was wrong with the team."

The constant pressure to win slowly changed Worsley's happy outlook. Things no longer seemed as funny as they had in New York. "I never had trouble sleeping in New York," Worsley complained. "But after a couple of years with the Canadiens I had trouble. Then my wife started to beef that I was kicking out shots in my sleep and kicking her."

When the NHL expanded in 1967 the Canadiens had to make long coast-to-coast trips to meet their new Western rivals. Now Gump really had something to worry about. Although on the ice the veteran goalie seemed to be totally without fear, off the ice it was an entirely different story: Gump was absolutely terrified of flying!

"The first time I ever flew was in 1949 when I was with the New York Rovers and we took a plane home from a game at Milwaukee," Worsley said. "One of the engines caught fire, and we had to make an emergency landing in a field. Ever since then, I've been scared stiff in a plane."

"I couldn't believe anyone could be that frightened in a plane," said coach Blake. "Gump would be soaked with perspiration and clinging to the arms of his seat."

But even with the added pressures Worsley's play continued to improve. In 1967–68 he was chosen to the first All-Star team, maintained a 1.98 average to share the Vezina Trophy with Rogatien Vachon and led the Canadiens to another Stanley Cup with a 1.88 average in twelve playoff games. The Canadiens claimed still another Cup in 1969, and again Worsley was a key factor in their triumph.

Early in the 1969–70 season the Canadiens were flying from Chicago to Montreal when the plane hit an air pocket and dropped several hundred feet. The stewardess was serving dinner at the time, and the panic-stricken Worsley wound up covered with food. When the plane made a stopover in Toronto, Gump jumped off and took the train back to Montreal. The next day he suddenly announced his retirement, claiming his nerves were shot.

Late in the 1969–70 season Wren Blair, the general manager of the Minnesota North Stars, tried to convince Worsley that his career was far from finished. Blair assured the hesitant goalie that there would be much less pressure with the expansion North Stars than there had been with the contending Canadiens. Three months away from hockey and flying had settled Worsley's nerves, so he agreed to give Minnesota a try.

Worsley played eight games with the North Stars before the season ended. His exceptional goaltending helped provide a late surge, and Minnesota wound up with an unexpected playoff berth in the West Division.

Worsley enjoyed his brief stint in Minnesota, so he signed a contract for the 1970–71 season and moved his wife and three children to Minneapolis. He had a good year with a 2.49 average in 24 games despite a bothersome leg injury.

"The situation in Minnesota was ideal, very free of pressure," Worsley said. "Suddenly I was enjoying hockey again. I didn't mind flying quite as much, but I doubt if I'll ever really enjoy it."

**Worsley and some Minnesota teammates put the squeeze on the Maple Leafs' Jim Harrison (7).**

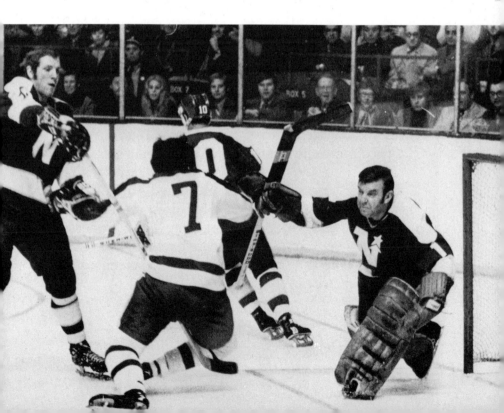

Worsley played some of the best goal of his career in the 1971–72 season as the North Stars challenged the powerful Chicago Black Hawks for first place in the West Division. He had an amazing 2.12 average in 34 games and returned to his old fun-loving style. He even abandoned his crewcut and allowed his hair to grow long enough to part. Just after the season ended, Worsley celebrated his 43rd birthday, which made him the second oldest player in the NHL. Another goalie, Toronto's Jacques Plante, was four months older.

"People always ask me how long I'm going to play," Worsley said. "Well, I don't know. As long as I can do the job, I guess, and I don't have any serious injuries. As I get older, I seem to feel the bruises a little more and the chance of pulling muscles increases.

"But if the rules committee would adopt my recommendation and outlaw shots on goal, I might play forever."

However, in January 1973, after several injuries, Worsley retired from the North Stars. He pulled a muscle in his thigh kicking out his pad to stop a shot, and the injury was very slow to heal. The Minnesota management tried to talk him into finishing the season, but Gump refused.

"The leg injury reduced my effectiveness," Worsley explained. "If I continued to play and wasn't able to give my best, then I'd be cheating my teammates."

# VLADISLAV TRETIAK
## Russia's Secret
## Weapon

Who's afraid of Vladislav Tretiak? Until September 1972, the answer to that question was "nobody!" Most hockey fans had never even heard of the Russians' number one goalie, and the few who had were hardly impressed. But when the Soviet National Team met the top NHL stars of Team Canada in the unofficial "world series" of international hockey, Tretiak almost stole the show.

Hockey had been played in the Soviet Union for many years, but it wasn't until the late 1940s that the country launched a serious program to prepare its players for world competition. The

135

**Vladislav Tretiak makes his North American debut as the Soviet National Team meets Team Canada in the 1972 series opener.**

Russians began their effort by acquiring every available Canadian hockey manual and studying films of the Montreal Canadiens' great scoring star, Maurice "Rocket" Richard.

Until 1954, hockey had been a Canadian game. Canada had dominated world amateur hockey even though its top 700 players were professionals and therefore ineligible. And the players in the professional National Hockey League were considered the best in the world.

But in 1954 the Soviets suddenly emerged to challenge Canadian supremacy in amateur play. Their National Team made the finals of the world championships at Oslo, Norway, where it met Canada's top team, the East York Lyndhursts, a Toronto industrial league team which was reinforced by several senior players. In the decisive game, the upstart Soviets whipped Canada, 7–2—a shocking defeat for Canadian hockey and the country which invented the game.

From 1954 to 1972 the Russians won eleven world tournaments and four out of five Olympic gold medals. There were no professional leagues in the Soviet Union, so the very best players were available for amateur play. But the fact remained that Canadian amateur players were no longer good enough to compete with the Soviets. Canada's last win over the Russians in a world tournament or Olympic match came in 1961.

For years the Canadians tried to get permission to use professional players in the world tournament, but their requests were denied. In 1970 a new rule was added that would have permitted nine former professionals to play on the Canadian team. But the rule was taken out at the last moment. In protest, the Canadian National Team withdrew from the world tournament and disbanded. Canadian hockey fans were particularly angry about the amateurism rule because they believed that the Soviet players were amateur in name only. It was common knowledge that the players devoted full time to hockey eleven months a year.

In 1972, after two years of negotiations, the Soviets finally agreed to send their "amateur" National Team against the professionals of the National Hockey League for an eight-game series. Hockey fans all over the world had long awaited the first confrontation between Canada's best professional players and the Soviet team that had dominated world amateur hockey. Although the Russians had made remarkable progress in hockey, most hockey experts expected the NHL stars to overwhelm the Soviets.

Because the series was scheduled for September, the Russian players, who were in training all summer, were sure to be in top condition. Autumn was the offseason in the NHL, however, and Team Canada would have only a three-week training camp to prepare for the series.

Still, the Canadians didn't seem very worried. They believed that they had the edge in several important areas—goaltending, shooting and body-checking. In addition, Team Canada had years of experience in tough NHL competition.

As things turned out, however, those so-called "edges" were really myths. Although the Soviets' splendid conditioning gave them one important advantage, they also proved to be the equal of Team Canada in many other departments.

138

The myth that the Russians had never developed a top netminder was exploded by a 20-year-old army lieutenant named Vladislav Tretiak. Time and again he turned back the amazed NHL stars, contributing more than any other Soviet player to the shocking success of the Soviet team.

During their domination of world amateur hockey, the Soviets had developed two good goalies, Vladimir Puchkov and Victor Konovalenko, but never a great one. Konovalenko, a cocky, acrobatic man who was nicknamed "Little Bear," displayed more competitive fire than goaltending technique but was very effective anyway.

Because Russians do not play baseball or any game that requires the catching of a ball, Soviet goalies tended to be weak with their glove hands. Most Russian goaltenders relied on reflexes rather than technique. But the Soviets were determined to overcome that weakness.

A national "crash program" aimed at the development of top goalies produced Vladislav Tretiak. The young goalie had played solidly but unspectacularly when the Russians won the Olympic gold medal at the 1972 Games in Japan. He was only mediocre in the '72 world tournament, and Czechoslovakia upset the Soviets to win the title.

The coach of the Czech National Team was unimpressed with Tretiak's performances. "We

**Tretiak poses with Soviet coach Tarasov (center) and veteran goalie Victor Konovalenko, "The Little Bear."**

felt Tretiak was one of the few weak spots on the Russian team," said Czech coach Stanislaus Kaskta. "He was very weak with his catching hand in the world tournament. But somehow, over the summer before he played the professionals, he learned to use it."

The Canadians, too, underestimated Tretiak. Before the series began, Team Canada sent Toronto Maple Leaf officials, coach Johnny McLellan and director of personnel Bob Davidson, to Russia to scout the opposition. They had no chance to watch the Soviet National Team perform as a unit, but they did get to see the individual players in action with their club teams during a summer tournament.

The night the scouts saw Tretiak perform with the Central Army Club of Moscow, he was badly beaten by the competition. McLellan and

Davidson reported that the Soviets could have problems because of Tretiak's poor performance. The Russians' second goalie, Vladimir Shepovalov, was injured, so Tretiak would have no help in goal.

"The night we saw Tretiak he gave up eight goals and looked awful," McLellan said. "He stopped nothing; he seemed to be in a fog."

What McLellan didn't know was that Tretiak had a good—and temporary—reason for that "fog." When the Russian goalie heard about the Canadian scout's opinion, he explained his poor performance. "That night was not one of my good nights, true," Tretiak said. "But you must understand that I was getting married the next day, and my mind was far away from the hockey match."

By the time the Soviet team arrived in Canada for the opening game of the series, Tretiak's fog had cleared. But watching the Soviets practice before the game, the Canadian players agreed with the scouts' first impression of Tretiak. They spotted what they considered flaws in the Russian's style, such as his stabbing at the puck with his stick. He seemed to be no match for the Team Canada goalies—Ken Dryden of Montreal, Tony Esposito of Chicago, and Eddie Johnston of Boston.

However, when the tension-packed first game started, such fabled Team Canada shooters as Phil Esposito, Frank Mahovlich, Yvan Cournoyer and Brad Park discovered that Tretiak was an excellent goalie. Wearing a "bird cage" face mask that resembled a baseball catcher's mask, the lanky (6-foot-1, 174-pound) goalie played an exceptional game as the Soviets scored a stunning 7–3 victory. Tretiak seldom fell to the ice and he moved out of the goal crease to challenge the big gunners the same way the best NHL goalies did. At the other end of the rink, Dryden had a miserable night as the well-conditioned Russian attackers poured through Team Canada's defense.

Tretiak continued to paralyze the NHL stars. The Canadians managed only one win out of the four games played in their own country. The Russians came up with two victories and one tie.

By the time the series moved to Moscow, the Canadian players had begun to regain their conditioning. Now it was Team Canada's turn to shine. After losing game five, Dryden and Tony Esposito played brilliantly in the final three games, all of which produced one-goal victories for the Canadians. Paul Henderson of the Toronto Maple Leafs fired the winning goals in each of the three games. In the eighth game, his winning marker came on a rebound after Tretiak had made a brilliant save on Henderson's first shot.

Team Canada had won the series, but they certainly did it the hard way. Henderson's final game-breaking goal came just 34 seconds before the end of the game. The highly-favored Canadians had squeaked through with four wins, three losses and one tie. Vladislav Tretiak was the man responsible for that close call, as the Canadians were quick to admit.

"Tretiak was just a good goalie, that's all," said Phil Esposito. "All the stuff we'd heard— and believed—about the Russian goalies? Well, Tretiak took about five goals away from me in the first game, and I started to wonder a little about the guys who had scouted him."

Tretiak played consistently well for the entire series. Although Team Canada out-shot the Russians in all games, at no point did Tretiak show signs of cracking under the pressure.

**Team Canada's Phil Esposito (left) is jubilant after finally scoring on Tretiak. Esposito found the young Russian a worthy opponent.**

"He didn't give up what we call a bad goal in the entire eight games," said Team Canada coach Harry Sinden.

Vladislav Tretiak was a fine example of the excellent athletes developed by the Soviet sports system. Born in Moscow in 1952, Tretiak developed his interest in hockey from his mother, who played "bandy," a kind of field hockey on skates that is similar to Canada's shinny.

At the age of seven, Tretiak began attending state-sponsored sports classes where he participated in several athletic activities—hockey, volleyball, basketball, soccer, tennis and gymnastics. His mental and physical abilities were examined by special physical training instructors in a program designed to find young Russian boys with athletic potential. When he was eleven years old, Tretiak's test results indicated that hockey was his best sport, and he joined the Central Army Club junior sports school in Moscow. The club had complete sports facilities and was the training site for many top Soviet athletes.

In many ways the young Russian was not very different from his North American counterparts, who played shinny on the frozen lakes of Canada. Vladislav, too, dreamed of stardom—not in the pro leagues, but on the highly regarded amateur National Team.

"I saw the colorful sweaters of the Central Army team, and I decided that I wanted a uniform like that some day," Tretiak recalled. "When I started in hockey I tried to be a forward, but then I slowly learned that goal was my best position."

As Tretiak developed into the best young goalie in Russian hockey, he was noticed by Anatoli Tarasov, the country's hockey genius and head coach of the Central Army Club team. It was Tarasov who had guided the Russian National Team to its dominant position in world amateur hockey.

Tarasov had carefully studied Canadian hockey, adopted its best features and added new wrinkles of his own. As a model goaltender, Tarasov selected Jacques Plante, the NHL wizard who had refined his craft to a science.

"Everything we Russians know about goaltending we picked up from Plante," Tarasov once said. "He was the best man to study because he knew everything about his position."

Tarasov spent many hours with Tretiak, drilling the young goalie on the fine points of the game. At the age of 16, Tretiak became the regular goalie on the strong Central Army team in the top Russian league. Tretiak also played with the victorious Soviet team in the 1968 European junior championships.

Tretiak earned a spot on the Soviet National Team in 1970. He helped the team to the world championships in 1970 and 1971 and the Olympic title in 1972. In the 1972 world tournament, the

Soviets lost to the Czechs in the finals.

Tretiak seemed to be having some trouble with his catching hand, and the National Team coaches Vsevelod Bobrov and Boris Kulagin developed a special program to strengthen it. When the Soviets began training in early June for the series against Team Canada, Tretiak participated in the club's long daily workouts. Then after each practice session, the young goalie spent hours in front of a machine that shot a puck at him every four seconds. It wasn't long before his catching hand improved.

"I also worked a long time each day with tennis balls for my reflexes and catching ability," Tretiak said. "I use two balls and I throw them at the wall, together or alternately, and catch them. I throw them as hard as I can and move closer to the wall."

Tretiak's efforts were well rewarded. His superior goaltending earned him a much higher standard of living than the average citizen in Russia, one of the benefits of "amateur" athletic achievement in the Soviet Union. His pay as a goaltending Army lieutenant was $488 per month, the equivalent of a general's salary. Tretiak also owned a car and had a large apartment, comforts of life denied to most Soviets his age.

Tretiak perfected his goaltending style by studying Konovalenko, watching films of the New York Rangers' Eddie Giacomin and talking with Jacques Plante. "From Konovalenko, I learned that a goalie must have self-confidence," Tretiak said, "and from Giacomin and Plante, I learned about goaltending techniques.

"I learned some things from watching Giacomin on film about how to play outside the goal crease and make it more difficult for the shooters. Jacques Plante was a very big help to me. In 1969 I toured Canada with the Russian team. Plante watched me in a practice at Montreal and passed along information on mistakes he saw me making."

Tretiak had obviously considered Plante a hero. The day before the first game of the Team Canada-Soviet series at Montreal, Plante presented Tretiak with a face mask, manufactured in Plante's factory in Quebec. With the help of an interpreter, the two goalies had a long discussion about playing goal.

Team Canada goalie Ed Johnston claimed that Plante's influence on Tretiak's style was easy to detect. "You can see Jacques' scientific approach in the way Tretiak plays," Johnston said. "He doesn't go down on the angles, and he turns with the play when an attacker cuts in front of the net, just the way Jacques does."

Plante was impressed with his unofficial student's progress. "I didn't really teach him that much, just a little about playing the angles and positioning himself in the net," he said. "Tretiak has to learn to use his stick a little more and how to control the puck with it in the goal area."

147

**Still wearing his "birdcage" face mask, Vladislav Tretiak relaxes after a hard-fought game.**

The results of Tretiak's hard work and study were clearly visible when he met the Canadians. Although Team Canada enjoyed a solid margin in shots on goal in most games, the Russians held a 32–31 edge in total goals during the series. In his eight games in the Soviet net, Tretiak continually frustrated the professionals with dazzling saves. To the astonishment of the Canadians, he had held the world's greatest shooters to a standoff. Hockey fans everywhere looked forward to seeing the young goalie again. Tretiak had learned his lessons so well that he seemed ready to teach the rest of the world a thing or two about tending goal.

148

# Index

*Page numbers in italics refer to photographs.*

149